THE BUDGET KIT

Fifth Edition

Other Books by the Author

The Money Tracker: A Quick and Easy Way to Keep Tabs on Your Spending

101 Great Ways to Improve Your Life, Volume 2 (contributing author)

The Family Memory Book: Highlights of Our Times Together

Daily Riches: A Journal of Gratitude and Awareness

Common Cent$: The Complete Money Management Workbook
(Forerunner to the current *Budget Kit*)

THE BUDGET KIT

Fifth Edition

The Common Cents Money Management Workbook

JUDY LAWRENCE

KAPLAN PUBLISHING

New York

Editorial Director: Jennifer Farthing
Acquisition Editor: Shannon Berning
Development Editor: Cynthia Ierardo
Production Editor: Fred Urfer
Cover Designer: Rod Hernandez

Published by Kaplan Publishing, a division of Kaplan, Inc.
1 Liberty Plaza, 24th Floor
New York, NY 10006

Printed in the United States of America

January 2008
10 11 12   10 9 8 7 6

ISBN 13: 978-1-4277-9672-1

Kaplan Publishing books are available at special quantity discounts to use for sales promotions, employee premiums, or educational purposes. Please email our Special Sales Department to order or for more information at *kaplanpublishing@kaplan.com*, or write to Kaplan Publishing, 1 Liberty Plaza, 24th Floor, New York, NY 10006.

DEDICATION

To my parents who inspired my skills and interest in managing money and ultimately my financial career through their everyday examples

CONTENTS

An inspirational story and practical suggestions for making major life changes.

An overview of the variety of worksheets available for getting the maximum benefit from this workbook. Also provides insight for handling savings, electronic budgeting, and family management of the budget.

Explore the expanding world of cashless transactions. Learn about options for online and electronic money management programs and how they fit with your current system. Find updates on credit reports and identity theft.

A place to record online bill payment schedules, website addresses, user IDs, passwords, password hints, and related information.

PART ONE

A picture of your total financial worth. A valuable aid for loan and insurance purposes.

A place to write your goals and a method to help you stay on target for reaching those goals.

A reminder of items or services that each family member needs and/or wants when extra money is available.

PART TWO

Monthly Expense Record **115**
> A record of all money earned and spent each month. A valuable tool
> for finding out exactly where your money is going. Very helpful when
> establishing a personal budget and deciding which expenses to reduce.

Summary-for-the-Year Record/End-of-the-Year Tax Information . . . 145
> A summary of each month's total income and expenses. Excellent
> for measuring your financial progress and making future plans.

PART THREE

Medical Expense Record **151**
> A record of mileage, dates, total bills, and reimbursements from
> insurance for visits to the doctor, hospital, drugstore, etc. Invaluable
> for tax time and personal records.

Flexible Spending Account Record **155**
> A record of all your reimbursable expenses.

Tax-Deductible Expense Record. **157**
> A convenient record of your various tax-deductible expenses, whether
> donations, professional dues, or taxes—all in one place for tax time.

Miscellaneous Expense Record **161**
> Place to keep additional records needed for taxes or personal use,
> such as automobile, child care, and education expenses, as well as
> casualty and theft losses.

Investment/Savings Record **165**
> A record of certificates of deposit (CDs), money market accounts,
> stocks, bonds, mutual funds, and other simple investments or savings.

Savings Activity Record. **170**
> A record of your monthly savings for your emergency, reserve, and
> goal funds. Also shows withdrawals and interest earned.

Retirement Savings Record **171**
> A record of your regular contributions to various retirement programs.

Child Support Records **173**
> A place to record necessary information related to child support,
> such as check number, amount, date, and arrival date.

Child Support Payment Record. **176**

Child Support Enforcement Record. **177**
> A record of all necessary information if you ever need help from the
> Child Support Enforcement Agency.

Child Visitation Record **177**

Subscription Record **179**
> A record of all subscriptions (trade journals, magazines, newsletters,
> etc.) so you know when you paid and can plan when to renew.

PREFACE

We've all heard the saying, "If it's not broke, don't fix it." That idea has certainly applied to this workbook, which has been around since 1981 when I originally self-published it as *Common Cent$*. Over the years, there have been minor revisions and additions to reflect the needs of the times.

Now, as this workbook continues in its third decade, a new millennium, and a world of high-speed Internet answers to everything, I am pleased to say that the core money-management concepts and worksheets provided in these pages are more timely and effective than ever. Even if you are starting to transition to financial software and online banking, you will find the overall budgeting process, the organized layout, and the comprehensive categories to be extremely helpful and transferable as you move to the electronic level of managing your finances.

In fact, one of the more timely features in this revised edition is the discussion of the "cashless society" concept—managing your financial affairs without actually directly handling any money. If you have been hesitant or confused about managing your finances electronically or online, my goal is to help you successfully maneuver your way into and through the maze of electronic and cyberspace choices, so you gain confidence and stay in financial control during this electronic transition.

Each revision, including this one, came as a result of many wonderful reader comments and suggestions, as well as my own seminar and one-on-one counseling experience with hundreds of clients over the years. I continue to welcome your recommendations for enhancing this workbook so it best fits your needs and helps you reach your goals.

My intention always was and still is to help you get started by providing a guideline or road map that is flexible enough to accommodate the many unique regional and personal situations as well as software packages that exist. The variety of worksheets throughout this workbook are designed to give you an overall and meaningful view of your monthly and yearly finances at a glance. Modify them as needed to fit your particular needs and lifestyle.

One woman looking at this workbook at one of my seminars asked, "Where's the theory?" The "theory" can be found in almost every personal finance book on the market. I'll bet you have a few of those books on your bookshelves right now. Most of these books discuss volumes of valuable financial information. For a list of helpful books and resources, see the

"Recommended Reading" and **"Online Resources"** sections in the back of this book. The authors usually encourage readers to establish a budget or spending plan and briefly discuss and show some examples. That still leaves the actual "doing it" part up to you, and that's usually where the procrastination, confusion, or fear sets in.

If you haven't been taught how to manage money and set up a budget, how would you know what to do? Just having money does not necessarily guarantee your ability to manage it. Not everyone has the time, knowledge, or organizational skills to set up a simple, functional system for managing all their daily, monthly, and yearly finances. That's why I designed and wrote this down-to-earth, realistic workbook. Instead of theory, the *focus of this workbook is to complement the other financial books and give you a tool you can pick up, quickly read, and easily and confidently start to use at any time by just gathering your financial papers, pencil, calculator, and eraser.*

As a counselor, I originally designed this workbook for young families and for women who were suddenly widowed or divorced, had limited money-management skills, and who often were intimidated by the whole idea of dealing with money. I have since realized, through my seminars, clients and from the many letters and phone calls I have received from people of all professions and incomes, that managing finances is a universal concern.

In fact, don't feel you are alone if managing your finances during these times as an individual or a couple is feeling like a real challenge. Even though our technology and education has become more sophisticated, more and more of my clients are professional attorneys, accountants, bank VPs, coaches and more. All are trying to weave their way through the endless financial and personal responsibilities and challenges of today's fast paced and demanding life styles and find peace and clarity in the process.

What I also have seen become a major universal concern over the years is consumer debt. What an irony this seems to be after so many prosperous years of some of the lowest unemployment numbers, greatest economic growth, and highest investment returns this country had ever experienced. If there was ever a time you would think debt would have been at an all-time low, it would have been during the boom years. But debt levels did not go down then, and debt now continues to be at an all-time high.

Another major financial issue facing consumers is the fallout of the popular adjustable rate interest-only mortgages. Consumers did not factor in future economic changes and rising interest rates, nor did they factor in the impact this would have on their budgets. During the next few years, as more people deal with foreclosures and bankruptcies, the need for effectively managing personal finances and personal debt is stronger than ever. The **"Debt Payoff Record"** section of this workbook is designed to help you manage your debt and motivate you to get out of debt. Through this worksheet, you can see at a glance your successful progress toward financial independence and financial control as you pay down, and ultimately off, your debt.

Once you take the time to start organizing and planning your financial affairs with these worksheets, the results will be extremely rewarding. Remember, this workbook is a tool for you to use. By itself, it will not change anything. *With your input and your consistent and thorough participation in setting your goals, planning your expenses, recording and paying attention to your spending, and utilizing the many valuable sections, this workbook will help you create magic with your finances.*

The magic will be in the form of financial peace of mind replacing financial chaos. Bill paying will be more manageable and automatic, which alone will save hundreds of dollars from late-fee expenses. If you are ready to start paying bills online, you'll be guided through that as well. Getting into the savings habit will be easier and more rewarding as you use the different savings records and watch your balances grow. Tax time will flow more smoothly when you use the tax-deduction records and have all the information you need at your fingertips. Keeping child support records will be more effective with the guiding worksheets. These records could provide that extra edge or make the deciding difference if you ever need to go back to court and verify any information.

And, finally, life will take on a whole new meaning when your stress level around money is greatly reduced and at last there is room for those other aspects of your life to come back into focus and balance.

Over the years, many of my readers have told me about the new sense of balance and control they were able to achieve by using this workbook. It has been extremely gratifying for me to learn how readers were able to purchase their first home, save their marriage, get out of debt, and start saving and investing money for the first time. Using this workbook has literally changed lives. I look forward to hearing how it changes yours. I wish you a successful and prosperous year.

"Being recently divorced and new to managing money, I was surprised to find that doing these steps actually energizes me! When I write everything down and have a plan, I find I am no longer worrying about it. It really makes a difference!"

Prologue

As I finished a previous revision of *The Budget Kit* and prepared to mail it to the publisher, a very special friend stopped me and said the book was not yet complete. She told me I needed to share my story of how I recently made a major mental, emotional, and geographical shift in my life and ultimately landed in my own paradise. After some consideration, I agreed.

My goal for my readers and clients always has been to uplift, encourage, and instill hope and confidence. From the response I received to this prologue, I knew I had touched a special chord for people. I hope the following story will inspire you to make whatever changes in your life you feel that you need to step into your own dreams.

Going from the Desert to the Valley

Sometimes when things just don't seem to flow, and more and more of life seems like a struggle, I have learned it is time to stop and reflect. That time had come for me by the late nineties. Living in Albuquerque, New Mexico, was always a wonderful experience. The climate, uniqueness and beauty of the land, fulfilling friendships, and my professional budget counseling practice all were very satisfying to me. I never thought that I would someday want to leave or—more precisely—*have to* leave to really begin to thrive and move way beyond just surviving physically, emotionally, and financially.

I slowly began to realize that having loving friends, incredible respect in the professional community, and amazing hikes statewide, somehow were not filling me up. As one wise woman recently put it, I was continually on simmer in life, but never getting to the rolling boil. I had lived in the "desert"—and a beautiful desert—for more than 20 years and started to feel like I had taken the desert into my cells. Having grown up in the green lands and blue lakes of Wisconsin, I realized my whole being was starving for the lushness of green and water again—as well as the lushness of creativity, innovation, and passion.

Somehow much of my life had taken on the aspects of the desert. My clients came to me with issues of lack. As much as I loved working with them (and know I have impacted their lives in a tremendously positive way), it was becoming apparent that I was continually being around the concept of lack in my work life. As I hiked the foothills of the Sandia Mountains every morning, I took in the real physical lack that is represented by the desert landscape. When there is not a lot of moisture, plants learn to hang on to what little rain they get and adapt the best way they can. That means their branches, stems, and leaves all have a stiffness, starkness, and brittleness to them as they conserve what little moisture they have to stay alive.

I was seeing this same analogy in my professional world. My clients, with limited funds and limited options for bringing in more money (New Mexico had been ranked 48 in per capita income for many years), found the most effective strategy for their families was to hang on, cut back, and conserve whatever way they could. As practical as that approach is, and as often as we have been taught the technique of "spend less or earn more" from all directions, I believe there are times and places when the toll of that approach is too high. You soon start to believe that life is only like a desert and start to forget that many other landscapes exist. And even when you start to realize that other landscapes do exist, the thought of what it would take to get there can be way too overwhelming or scary. So you live life on a continual low simmer and never really get to that boil stage of abundance, opportunity, choices, and vitality.

Change—Terror or Liberation?

Getting to that other stage would require change. Change, for the majority of us, is extremely challenging and frightening. And so, once again, staying with the familiar continues to have more appeal. That is, until the familiar becomes more uncomfortable and unbearable than the fear of the unknown.

I had reached that point. For three years I knew, on some level, I needed to make major changes in my life. And I resisted. So many things I tried just never fully panned out. Gregg Levoy in his book *Callings: Finding and Following an Authentic Life,* talks about those callings, or messages. He tells stories of people taking up to five years before paying attention to what they needed to hear. That was helpful for me to know.

My turning point came when I woke up at 3 AM in a Chicago hotel in a panic attack. What was I going to do? The savings were going down even though I was a master at managing my money. The industry I was in was dramatically changing. There was no dependable, steady money coming in. The big chunks immediately got stashed for the lean times. I never felt I could really plan ahead. There was not a partner in my life to help support me emotionally, physically, or financially. I was not getting younger, even though I was blessed with good genes and excellent health.

"You do not get out of a problem by using the same consciousness that got you into it."

— Albert Einstein

How often I had heard the popular 12-Step definition of insanity—doing the same thing over and over and expecting different results. I knew I was living my life in the same place, basically the same way, with a few attempted changes, and wanting different results—a different life. I knew I had to change my life, but how? I was afraid to loosen the grip on any money I did have out of fear of not having any more coming in. At 3 AM there was no one to call as I sat in that dark hotel room in total despair.

Then the answer started to formulate. Guidance was coming through. I had a check coming to me that week and I knew I had to use that money to propel me in my new direction as soon as possible. The money would not be used for one more month of mortgage and the usual bills as that would only keep the same old pattern in place. I had been thinking about moving to the Silicon Valley in California after a friend had planted the seed in my mind two years earlier telling me stories about the start-ups and stock options. Words I didn't even understand. I knew then I had to go there and immerse myself in the middle of that energy of abundance.

The planning began for taking a quick trip. I had a friend there I knew would help me out, but what about the expense of the rental car, flight, and meals? The next day I called that friend, Carol, who graciously extended her home to me for three weeks. By the end of that day she called me to say her friends wanted me to house-sit their beautiful home while they were on vacation and to feel free to use their car. The magical flow had begun. I always knew to trust when everything starts to fall into place easily. Next I called the Career Action Center and offered to volunteer for three weeks. I knew I needed to live as if I was living there and having a place to go every day. I now had a plan.

Welcome to the Valley

Two weeks later I was in Cupertino, California. It didn't take me long to realize I had just gone from Sleepy Hollow to the Epicenter of the Galaxy. I had arrived at the height of the dot-com boom. The energy was off the charts. The traffic jammed. The housing and rental prices were too outrageous to even begin to think about. And still, I knew I had found my home. This was where I belonged.

Whatever it took, I knew I had to make the move. I had to totally change my life. It didn't matter that my computer skills were very limited. It didn't matter that my knowledge of technology was even more limited. Like a moth zooming to the light, I was choosing to head to the mother lode of computers and technology. If someone had told me I would move to Silicon Valley someday, I know I would have thought they were crazy. No way. Why move to the heart of the rat race? Yet there I was. I returned to Albuquerque and immediately put my condo up for sale in a market that was losing money. Next, I started going through stuff. It was time to clear out and move out!

Letting Go

I realized I couldn't get a *new* life if I kept holding on to all my *old* stuff. When planes are overweight with cargo, they can't take off from the runway and fly to the next destination. They need to clear out some baggage. And so I cleared 20 years of files and piles, drawers, closets, bookshelves, rooms, and my office. I let go of old patterns of hanging on to everything, whether for future use or recycling, attitudes that no longer served me, meetings and organizations that were no longer a fit for me. I got rid of furniture, appliances, my bed, and even my car. Time to buy a different car. The furniture and appliances could all be replaced. I had let go of my attachment to things. By the time I did move out in the fall of 1999, I left behind one very small but full storage shed, a few things at friends' homes, and took with me whatever could fit in my car.

That was not all that I took with me. Most important, I knew I was taking the essence of who I was. And that was the most valuable asset of all.

So what did I finally do about that outrageous housing market? I knew if I went down that path, I would be so terrified of the prices I would never leave my bed. Instead I decided to be financially creative. I put the word out everywhere before and after I moved that I would house-sit. Over four months I managed to house-sit in a variety of places in between staying with my friend Carol. By the last house-sitting arrangement, not only was I living rent free in a beautiful home with a pool once again, but I was getting paid well to feed Toots, the cat.

"What the mind can believe and conceive it can achieve."

— William James

Thinking Outside the Box Brings Dividends

So what was the key for me? During that whole process of knowing I needed to change right through to the point when I was determined to leave, I walked every morning along the foothills watching in my mind the video of the life I wanted to have. In my visionary world, the environment was sunny, lush, green, and fragrant. My workday consisted of doing satisfying work, making great money, and being part of a team of delightful, supportive, fun, bright, creative coworkers. People in general had an attitude of cooperation, appreciation, acceptance, diversity, creativity, potential, possibility, and vitality. The vision also included weekends of feeling the spray of the warm water as I slalom skied and enjoying the taste of the exquisite flavor of the salmon or trout on the houseboat trip. My energy level was high and sustained. I was happy, laughing a lot, thoroughly enjoying every experience and in total daily gratitude. In my core, I knew I was in total alignment and balance in my life.

To support this vision, I paid attention to all the signs around me whether from conversations, movies, books, birds, sounds, or even license plates. My journal is full of entries of one unbelievable synchronistic event after another. My condo sold to a perfect buyer. Money kept coming from unexpected sources. Offers of placement for storing or buying my things conveniently came to me. Everything flowed once I had made a clear decision to move.

Now, years later as I look back at this experience, I realize the true depth of this shift I had gone through as I processed those many lessons of life. Not only had I cleared out the external material clutter, but more significantly, the internal mental and emotional clutter. Once I was in this pure space, I was able to tap into my true authentic self, balance my head with my heart, and trust the results that would come.

This also explains more clearly why everything flowed once I had made that decision to move. Being in a pure inner space was the critical first step as I started creating the vision and the feeling of the life I really desired during those morning foothill walks.

When I originally wrote this story, I had lived in the Silicon Valley for only seven months. I absolutely loved it and was living most of my vision. I was a total match to the people and the creativity that surrounded me. The learning curve was extremely steep. As a very non-technical person, I still managed to start working at an Internet company. I finally understood and appreciated the term "lifelong learning." I was pedalling as fast as I could to get up to speed with computers, the Internet, and technology in general. Through it all, I was blessed with patient, supportive people all around me who continually guided me through the next new learning speed bump.

Home at Last

Now, years later, I have lived in the heart of Silicon Valley—the center of boom times and dot-com crash times. During those years I experienced my own version of financial boom and challenge. Yet, I can honestly still say this was the best move I ever made. I am still surrounded with an abundance of cooperation, appreciation, diversity, creativity, innovation, and possibility.

My nephew Dan once said, "Come to California and you will find what you are looking for." He was right. I did. Now, I remind myself to not put energy into regretting that I waited so long to take this risk or that I put so much energy into worry and fear for so many years. Over the years, I have learned to trust in divine timing. It's like the saying, "Taste no wine before its time."

A Financial Plan of Action for Change

I now encourage you to trust your own inner knowing. May my story or the following seven suggestions help you as you take your next step toward making a major change in life:

1. Find the balance between letting go and holding on. Letting go can mean relaxing your grip on your money, material possessions, ideas, or attitudes. It may mean a new found sense of generosity or desire for service. Finding that balance means learning how to discern when it feels better to finally let go or when it feels more appropriate to hold on to your money, possessions, or behavior patterns and respectfully manage what you do have.

2. Create a vision of what you want. Dr. Fred Waddell uses his "miracle question." If you were to wake up tomorrow and, by some miracle, your life was everything you ever wanted, what would it be like? How would it look, feel, sound, smell, and be? How would you live your life? Who would be in your life? What would you change? What would stay the same? Dream up your magical scenario and write it down.

3. Find a moment every day to spend time with your vision. Nothing new here. I'm sure you have taken the classes and read the books on creating visions and making goals a reality. This time how will you actually do that? A daily walk, morning mediation, regular journaling? How will you incorporate the different senses as you step into this vision every day?

4. Start letting go of the "stuff." Clear the clutter in your life. Donate, give to others, have yard sales, toss. Do whatever it takes to start shifting the energy and begin the process of change.

5. Explore new experiences. Take new classes, meet new people, try new hobbies, sports, crafts, books, CDs, websites. Change your routine. Expand your life.

6. Move. Sometimes our lives can take on a whole new perspective by geographically being someplace new. Move to a new home or a different part of the town, your state, or even the country. Travel to different places. I read an article about the importance of a "latitude adjustment." Geography really does affect many people. I know that is why foreign travel always feels good for me.

7. Use the tools and techniques in this workbook to build your savings. Using practical tools is one way to stay grounded and take personal responsibility for your life. Having savings provides security, freedom, and choices. As one friend put it, "When I have 'drop dead' money in savings, I have the freedom to leave any job any time without having to compromise my integrity." Following the guidelines in this workbook will help you create that freedom and ability to step forward into your vision.

May you too find the right time and the right guidance for creating and attaining whatever changes you desire in your life.

Many blessings,
Judy Lawrence

Introduction
How to Use *The Budget Kit*

"This workbook took some of the fear out of money for me. By setting up an amount I knew I could spend in an area, I didn't feel so bad when I was spending that money. I knew it was planned and okay. Before I was always in fear or guilt over everything I spent, thinking I was overspending."

The Purpose of this Workbook

The Budget Kit is designed to be easy to understand and practical to use. Because it is flexible, it can be used immediately regardless of the time of year or the condition of your finances. By following the guidelines in this workbook, you will learn to take charge of your overall finances by anticipating your monthly and yearly expenses, instead of always reacting to crisis after crisis.

There are two purposes for this workbook. The first is to help you keep proper records and get your financial information organized. With this workbook, you can keep records of your daily, monthly, and yearly payments and expenses, medical costs, installment payments, credit card charges, mail order and online purchases, child support payments, savings, investments, retirement income, and much more.

The second purpose is to help you successfully plan and manage your finances. You can list and plan your goals; work out an estimating method for paying yourself (savings), your bills, and your monthly expenses; remind yourself of items you need or want to buy when extra money is available; and plan ahead for the periodic, but anticipated, expenses throughout the year.

You will probably notice the brief discussion on many of the financial topics mentioned throughout this workbook. This brevity was deliberate, so the primary focus could remain on moving forward with action steps using the worksheets. Each financial topic already has volumes of books and websites available for more in-depth information.

How to Get Started

Set aside a block of time so you can thoroughly review the variety of sections available in this workbook. These sections contain instructions along with worksheets that were designed to address many different needs. Each worksheet can be used independently, with another, or as a setup guideline to use with any software you are using. Determine your own needs and see how this workbook will best fit them.

The many helpful worksheets in *The Budget Kit* are divided into three parts.

Part One helps you focus on where you are and where you want to be financially. Your *initial* time involved may be greater here as you gather and fill in the information. After completing this step, these pages become more of a place to revisit for reviewing and reflecting as the year goes on.

If this section feels a little overwhelming at this time, or you are very anxious to get started and want to jump right in and set up a spending plan, then move on to Part Two. Take a moment to skim through this first section and then come back later and complete it when it feels right for you.

Part Two is your action section where you plan, project, and record on a daily, monthly, and yearly basis. The bulk of your time and attention throughout the year will be spent in Part Two. You quickly will see how to anticipate those "unexpected" bills throughout the year, know how to plan out each month in advance, and learn where all your money is going.

All of this information and the way it is organized will be just as valuable if you are starting to manage your finances electronically.

Part Three is a collection of a variety of record-keeping worksheets for accommodating different individual needs. This is where you can keep records concerning child support income, mail orders, subscriptions, investments, retirement, savings, and other miscellaneous information. You also can record such expenses as medical and dental (including insurance reimbursements) as well as tax deductions.

Take some time to look through all three parts and the worksheets in each part, and see which ones will be more helpful for your particular financial situation.

Prepare for the Known, the Unknown, and your Dreams

By setting up your system for the year, you are planning ahead and getting a full financial picture. It won't be long before you see that you will need to have some system for saving money ahead of time for different purposes. Listed below are three different areas of savings I recommend you have.

1. Reserve account (the *known* expenses). After listing your major anticipated periodic or non-monthly expenses throughout the year on your **Yearly Budget**

Worksheet in Part Two (such as car insurance, home improvement plans, tuition, gifts, etc.), total these up. See the sample on *page 52.*

Divide this total number by 12 to calculate the monthly amount you need to set aside in a bank, credit union, or money market account for a reserve account. *Remember, this is not your emergency money. This is a savings for money that will be coming due, but at various times of the year.*

By setting this money aside each month, you will feel like you magically have extra money available when some of the bigger expenses (such as a family vacation, property taxes, or graduation) come due. These infrequent expenses no longer will disrupt your whole monthly budget or land on your credit card.

Enter this reserve savings category and the amount on your **Monthly Budget Worksheet** in Part Two under "Fixed Amounts" at the top part of the page. (See *page 67* for a sample.) Consider this part of "paying yourself first" as one of the fixed bills you pay each month.

2. Emergency account (the *unknown* expenses). There are going to be times when unknown disasters occur that create emergencies. Some examples are when the car breaks down, the home heating system needs to be replaced, your job position is eliminated, or your dental bridgework breaks.

The best way to have some peace of mind through any of these events is to know you have funds set aside in case an emergency occurs. The guideline amount has been to have three to six months' worth of take-home pay available. Save this money in a bank, credit union, money market account, or mutual fund with check writing privileges.

Determine what amount you can realistically save each month (you may want to use payroll deductions) and slowly build this account up. Enter this monthly saved amount under "Fixed Amounts" on the **Monthly Budget Worksheet** in Part Two. (Again, see the sample on *page 67.*)

Remember this money is *not* to be confused with the reserve account, which actually is being saved for expenses that have already occurred or will occur.

3. Goals account (your *dream* account). An entire section in Part One is devoted to identifying goals and saving for them. This is the third amount that will be included under the "Savings" category in the "Fixed Amounts" section on the **Monthly Budget Worksheet** in Part Two. Initially, this number may be a much smaller amount or even nonexistent until the other two accounts get started and have sufficient totals available.

By including your Reserve, Emergency, and Goals Accounts on the **Monthly Budget Worksheet**, you have a way of putting together and seeing your total spending plan. *This process also reminds and encourages you to save and put funds aside regularly, offering you a system for staying in control of your finances.*

Getting a Handle on Savings

If saving money is new for you, or has been difficult in the past, remember the most important part of this process is *starting*. If you can only start with $10 to $20 per pay period or per month in the beginning, that's okay. Start with that amount. Use automatic payroll deductions to make this habit easier for you. The significance of this monthly step is that you are establishing a very critical habit as well as starting to accumulate some savings. Don't be discouraged with the small amount in the beginning. When you keep up the saving habit, the balance in your savings will gradually grow. As you develop a more effective budget, the specific amount you are able to save each month also will start to grow.

Learning to plan and act proactively for the future will also serve you well the next time you receive a bonus or other lump sum of money. You will have more tools to discern how to utilize that money so it truly aligns with your overall goals and priorities, instead of just spending it mindlessly and spontaneously.

Remember to be realistic about the amount you can actually save in the beginning. Saving a small amount each month and leaving it in savings is much more productive financially and psychologically than depositing large amounts only to have to take money back out of savings each month to cover expenses. I have seen numerous clients with failed savings attempts and eroded confidence levels due to ambitious savings intentions, but with no backup spending game plan. Every time these clients withdrew money from their savings for basic living expenses, they were sabotaging themselves by subconsciously confirming their belief that they really can't save money. Once these clients developed a budget using many of the sections in this workbook, their savings plan stayed intact and grew in value. So did their confidence level. One couple depends on the routine of planning meetings to keep their household of five flowing smoothly.

"Every Sunday night when the kids are in bed, we sit down and talk about the finances. We make decisions about expenses and decide if we should spend money on something or save it."

Who Manages the Family Budget

Who handles the finances in your household? Often one partner assumes and maintains the role of "Family Budget Director." Many couples fall into their respective roles because they are good at it, like it, or have more time, or by default when one spouse refuses. These roles often can be logical and efficient provided that the "Family Budget Director" is good at managing money. Once this pattern is set, it can last for years, unless some event causes the routine to change.

I highly recommend that each spouse be involved with the household finances in some way, even if that means trading off partial or full-time responsibility every six months, every year, or every other year. By getting involved with your household finances on some regular basis, you develop an awareness of your financial obligations, limitations, spending patterns, and overall current financial status. You also have a better appreciation of how expenses are going up—especially if you have a very active, athletic (and hungry) teenager. For example, the rising price of groceries and kids' shoes becomes very apparent.

This awareness is especially important for personal relationships. There may be times when occasionally the partner managing the finances must announce: "No, we can't afford that item or luxury right now." That news can easily conjure up a whole gamut of reactions for the uninvolved partner. Feelings of confusion and misunderstanding can translate into: "What do you mean? We were just paid three days ago. What are you doing with all the money?!"

If that person who blew up had first-hand experience with the bills and budget for the past six months, it would be easier to see the reason for the decision to cut back. It is difficult to know what you really can and cannot afford each month when you start losing that total sense of what it costs to run your household. You may not be as in touch with how school functions and last minute events seem to gobble up the discretionary cash, how computer interests or other electronic games and devices tend to get more expensive, and how household repairs just manage to keep on piling up.

This mutual awareness by both partners is especially important if the designated Family Budget Director is suddenly in an accident or dealing with a long-term incapacitating illness in the hospital or suddenly dies or leaves due to a divorce. If the other partner is already familiar with the financial picture and the location of all the papers and records, then the trauma of the loss will not be compounded by the fear of taking on the new, often terrifying responsibility of handling all the finances.

Even without the traumatic circumstances, I have found many partners who confide that carrying this responsibility of having to make all the financial decisions alone for many years becomes a major emotional burden. Many times both partners are very relieved when I suggest that the responsibility be shared.

I strongly encourage couples to work together or trade off the responsibility of paying the bills and keeping records. Decide what works best for your situation and then follow through on that decision.

Family Affair

Financial discussions are also important to share with the whole family. Remember, you are being the financial role model for your children. You can do this deliberately or by default. One way to look at this is to ask yourself: "If my children were now adults and handling their money pretty much the way I do right now, would I be proud of how they were doing?" This question is more about a reality check and less about self-judgment.

Once you include the children in the decision process, you will be amazed at what insights they have to offer and how willing they are to cooperate.

If you are wondering how to get started, think of your family as a small business and consider having a weekly "family financial board meeting" on a regular fixed schedule. Set up the ground rules so everyone knows this is a safe and supportive place and time to express their thoughts and questions. It is a time for them to know they will be heard, not interrupted or put down. Establish an agenda where you will do your planning for the next week.

The following ideas are suggestions for how to productively use this family meeting time:

- Review your goals.
- Outline your spending choices and decisions.
- Determine charitable giving.
- Find creative ways to resolve money shortages or to utilize extra funds.
- Work out logistics of who will handle certain responsibilities.
- Be sure to acknowledge all the progress you have made as a "team" so far.

After a few months, or even weeks, you will begin to notice subtle changes everywhere—not just with the finances. Notice the shift in the family relationships, how the household is running, and the status of your checkbook balance.

When to Budget Electronically

In this Information Age where nearly everyone has a computer or computer access and answers can be delivered in seconds, you may feel compelled to use a financial software package to start your new budget. From my own experience with clients, I have learned that if you are new to budgeting, starting off with a new financial software package often is *not* the best way to begin—*especially if you have never created a budget, or successfully budgeted before.* I encourage you to know yourself and your style first. Think about the following four questions:

1. Do you work better when you see all the detail in one big picture? If so, then scrolling around a screen and moving to different screens to pull the whole picture together may feel more confusing or overwhelming when you are just learning the basic concepts of budgeting and money management. Instead, looking at an entire year or whole month-at-a-glance page in this Budget Kit workbook may suit your style more comfortably.
2. Are you impatient? Many people just want to get started and don't have the patience to learn all the options available on the software programs. I see many Quicken users who haven't utilized anywhere near all the handy tools available to them. Consequently, they are not getting all of the benefits or information that they could. In the meantime, they are entering figures and seeing reports, yet are not truly learning or understanding effective budgeting skills or concepts or even creating a realistic budget. I often find with new clients that they are using popular

software programs, but can't figure out why their spending plans are not working for them.

3. Do you tend to procrastinate? Turning on the computer, getting into the program, and entering the data may all become convenient deterrents for getting started or for keeping current. Some people find it easier to open this workbook, enter information, and be done. Again, think about how you operate and how often, when, and where you are on the computer.

4. Are you computer savvy? If you are, there is probably little that would convince you to write down information manually in the beginning when starting a budget. However, that is exactly what I am going to suggest if you are just starting to learn the concept of budgeting.

Even though you may feel you will get the same results by using your trusty computer, I have found that for many people there is critical tactile and visual learning that occurs with the manual approach that does not happen as effectively electronically. *As you physically write down the numbers and visually note them and the surrounding information, there is a special sensory awareness and understanding that occurs.* After using this method for a few months and dealing with the planning and recording of the unique variations of some of those months, you will have gained valuable insight and understanding.

Couples have told me that something seemed to be lost when they shifted from manual recording to the computer approach too early. The planning, inputting, and visual awareness changed somehow. Instead, they had reams of reports and averages, yet did not feel they had answers.

Electronic budgeting does work very well, however, when started at the right time. Once the overall concept is experienced and understood and you see how the smaller monthly and day-to-day pictures fit into the bigger yearly picture, then almost any method will work.

Transitioning over to a software package at *this* point does make sense—especially when the computer does all the calculations for you. You also can take advantage of other conveniences, such as printing checks, banking online, paying bills online, and numerous other services.

One obvious reminder if you do convert exclusively to financial software or some online program through the Internet is to keep backup paper records or always have current backup on CDs or external hard drive as a protection against any unexpected computer crash.

Take Charge of Your life and Money

The methods and guidelines in this workbook will show you how to set your goals, watch your spending, plan your expenses, and save more money. You then will find that your bills are paid on time, more money is saved than you ever thought possible, your investments are off to a healthy start, your goals are being reached, and the stress in your life is reduced.

As you take charge of your money, you will notice this control carrying over to other aspects of your life. Your relationships with your family will become more relaxed and more time will be available to pay attention to other things in life besides money.

Most importantly, you will begin to notice a new awareness of your priorities and values. *Paying attention to your finances in a more conscientious and deliberate way will help you see that your actions, beliefs, and results are in total alignment with your true life priorities and values.*

Best of luck as you begin your new money-management journey!

Living in a Cashless Society

The future of a cashless society, heralded for so many years, is now here and not going away. Whether you fully embrace the Internet and the convenience of managing all your financial affairs electronically and online, or participate unconsciously by regularly using your ATM, debit card, and credit card or by actively resisting going cashless, preferring your tangible cash and checks, it's time to understand how the cashless society will affect your life.

Already, you may go through a day, a week, or a month without ever actually touching, exchanging, or seeing cash or checks. How does this method of operating with "invisible money" affect how you create and/or maintain a successful spending plan?

For some, it has already become a nightmare as they try to manually balance various checking accounts and track multiple credit and debit cards to get a handle on how much is actually being spent. Without extreme discipline and a plan, it is nearly impossible to gather up and record, with any accuracy, all the loose pieces of financial information rolling away in unrecorded multiple ATM withdrawals, debit payments (plus the requested extra cash), and automatic bank withdrawals.

For others, who immediately appreciated the potential of the cashless option, heaven has just arrived on earth. At last, they feel organized and efficient, have a convenient system that works, and know exactly where they stand financially at any given time.

How is this stream of plastic, electronic, and online options affecting your own financial situation?

What Is a Cashless Society?

Every financial transaction you make that does not involve an exchange of actual cash or a written check essentially is a cashless transaction. The more familiar examples of electronic, cashless transactions traditionally used for years are credit and charge cards, debit cards, direct deposit, and direct payment. As the online process and wireless possibilities continue to evolve, these cashless transaction options will seem endless.

Let's consider some of the many different ways we now operate in a society without the use of cash.

Online Shopping. One familiar example, online shopping, has been around for years. However, now we make payments for online shopping with money out of a checking account, without writing a check or even using a debit card. In the same way, you can safely receive payments from individuals through private online e-payment services. PayPal®, the most familiar online e-payment service as of this printing, provides an online alternative to using credit cards for consumers making online purchases or depositing funds received. They are notified of the transaction confirmations through email. These new online payment changes emerged when online auctions blasted onto the Internet scene.

Prepayment Cards. Another cashless transaction example is the convenience of the prepayment cards (also called reloadable or reup cards) for upcoming purchases or services such as coffee shops, bookstores, copy centers, washer/ dryers, phones, public transit, and numerous other services. You can add specific dollar amounts to prepayment cards by using your credit card or transferring money from your bank.

HELOC Cards. Another cashless option becoming more popular is the HELOC (home equity line of credit) card, which operates just like a credit card. The general idea is to charge expenses and pay off the balance in full each month. Using this card only for emergencies is prudent. *Getting into the habit of using the equity of your home as your backup when making mundane purchases like groceries and gasoline is downright dangerous. Moving in this direction is a bit like deciding to feast on the goose that was laying the golden eggs.*

Online Banking. And finally, the ultimate in going cashless and paperless is using online banking. This service provides all the functionality of your corner bank, such as opening a checking and savings account or money market account, transferring money between accounts, viewing transactions and current balances, taking out loans, and opening investment accounts. In addition, you have the ability to receive and pay all your bills online, which goes beyond the basic, traditional automatic bank payment for loans, utilities, and insurance that was available for so long. More and more of these online and cashless services will become available for solving the next obstacle that keeps you and your money from getting to the product or service of your choice.

The Internet has revolutionized how we live and manage our financial lives. You may not currently be part of this financial online revolution, but it won't be long until banking online will be as much a part of your life as using the ATM is now.

According to an October 2005 Forrester Research study, by 2010, over half (52%) of online households will pay bills online. This is a 75% increase from 2005. It is an even greater increase from the time this section of the workbook was originally written. This same study expects the number of Generation Y consumers (born 1976–1990) paying bills online to increase 219%. Clearly, we are moving our finances online.

The question once again is, How are these innovative financial changes impacting your life and your own financial management system or spotlighting your *lack* of a system?

Are You Ready to Enter Cyberspace, or Already There?

You may have joined the ranks of computer-savvy individuals who now comfortably navigate through cyberspace. Maybe you grew up using the computer and the Internet. If so, using the concepts, categories, and formats in this workbook will supplement whatever electronic system or program you currently use or plan to use, and will help you develop a more effective spending plan.

On the other hand, are you sitting on the sidelines hoping that society will come to its senses and get back to the basics of cash? Or, have you been waiting to jump on this new Internet age rocket and and now want to take advantage of all these new services? Or are you still feeling a bit confused or intimidated about how or where to begin? If so, this section of *The Budget Kit* will be your Cliffs Notes for joining the online financial advancements of the 21st century. My goal is to support you and nudge you through the process of getting up to speed, so you can participate comfortably, confidently, and effectively in this continually emerging cashless world.

How to Get Up to Speed Electronically

If you have operated in a non-technical environment for many years and are just now entering the new electronic and online world, pay attention to the language being used by people more comfortable with technology. Part of the confusion is the language itself. New words are being used and introduced that are not even in dictionaries yet. Other words are being used to express processes and concepts you may actually understand, but the way the vocabulary has changed, it's easy to feel intimidated. Part of my goal here is to introduce you to various terms and expressions and help you better understand this new language.

Complete books have been written about this topic, and endless articles and websites exist, including bank websites and companies you now use, that explain this new technology in much more depth. There is no shortage of information available for you once you feel ready to move past this introductory stage.

Using Personal Finance Software

You've probably heard of Quicken software. In fact, this personal finance software was introduced around the same time as the original *Common Cents* (forerunner to *The Budget Kit*) workbook was published. You've also probably heard of another familiar software product called Microsoft Money. These two major, established personal finance software programs have been around the longest, offer the most features, and are supported by many of the larger banks.

Everything you have ever done manually is now conveniently available electronically—but with so many more features and possibilities. The standard services you can expect on these programs are:

- Banking
- Bank reconciliation
- Budget planning
- Bill paying
- Reporting
- Personal investing
- Tax options
- Financial planning

If your bank supports one of these programs, you can go to your bank account online and download (meaning, transfer information electronically) all the information automatically from your bank account into the software on your computer. This gives you the convenience of reconciling your bank and home accounts and recording your transactions, thus saving you the time and the effort of manually typing in all the transaction information.

If one of your primary objectives is to use a software program that helps you develop and manage an effective budgeting system, be sure the program offers an easy way to tie your spending to your income, and a way to know where you stand on a day-to-day basis in any particular spending category in your budget.

There are a number of personal finance software programs available to organize and manage your money and investment information. Even though these programs offer convenient records that show you where the money was spent, the information is *after the fact* and available only by going to the report section. Also, reports are only as accurate as the information you did or did not provide. When deciding on which personal finance software program to use, keep in mind your key objectives as well as your personal spending and recording style.

Information Needed for Purchasing Software

Review the four questions on *page* 6 under "When to Budget Electronically." Do your answers clearly show that it now makes sense for you to move to the electronic level? If so, let's look at what to consider before purchasing personal finance software.

System Requirements. If you don't have the technical language and understanding down yet, ask a friend to look at your computer system and tell you what your computer actually has. Then have them show you where to find this information. Does your computer have all the required amounts of hard drive space and memory, and an operating system that is needed to use the program? This information is listed on the outside of the package. Do you know what your operating system is, or what processor you have?

Ease of Use. Is this software program easy to set up initially? Can you catch on quickly to how the software works, either through the manual, tutorials on the software, or the intuitive visual simplicity of the software design? Once you are using the software, is it easy to use and input new records and information?

Functions Provided. Decide exactly what you want the software to do. Does the software actually do what you want it to do in terms of basic banking, budgeting, reporting, and bill payment? Is the information organized and presented in a way that is helpful to you? Is it easy to back up your information (meaning, a way to save all of your information on a CD or external hardware)? Are there more bells and whistles than you really want, making it confusing for you?

Available Help and Upgrades. What type of service is available when you have questions? Live assistance by phone? Prompts on the telephone? Online help? Do you have to pay for these services? Will you need to upgrade every year for your program to continue to run well? And if so, at what cost? Will those upgrades continue to be compatible with your current equipment?

Introduction to Online Banking

With ever-changing technology, many of the current online services will probably evolve significantly over the next few years. Presently, there are three main types of banks with a range of electronic options, from very limited to very comprehensive. The one you use depends on your personal style and needs:

- Brick and mortar. This is just a new way of referring to your traditional corner bank with the friendly tellers, coffee, express deposit drop-offs, and full line of financial services.
- Click and mortar (also called brick to click). This is the same as your corner bank ("mortar"), but this bank gives you the option to also manage your banking on your computer ("click") by using the Internet. Most large and regional banks offer fully functional online banking, so you can view all your accounts (including your CDs and IRAs) and check the balances and transaction history, make transfers, schedule future transfers, pay one-time or recurring bills, receive printable confirmations on all transactions, and have live 24-hour phone assistance.
- Virtual. You guessed it—there is no physical bank building. Virtual banks are the new breed of banks that offer the same range of banking services but are independent businesses and exist exclusively on the Internet. They still follow the same required federal banking regulations. Virtual banks appeal most to people who spend the majority of their work and personal time on the computer and online.

Online Bill Payment

When you're ready to venture beyond the initial online banking services, such as viewing your account balances, transaction history, checks that cleared, and making fund transfers, your next adventure will be to explore the online bill payment service. Once you really get comfortable with this service and experience the convenience of paying your bills each month with only a few clicks, you will probably be hooked and will be talking casually with family and friends about your "payee list" or "repeating payments" as comfortably as you now talk about email.

Three Ways to Pay Bills Online. There are a variety of ways to utilize online bill payment, but overall it boils down to three general options:

1. Your current bank. With most fully functional click-and-mortar banks, you can pay each bill as a one-time bill, set up payments for recurring bills, pay multiple bills at once, and even set up future periodic payments. Payments to small companies with no electronic service also can be handled. In some cases, banks (or a service they use) are literally writing physical checks to these small companies or individuals for you as a service, which is usually part of the nominal fee they may charge. Just as banks used to woo patrons with toasters in the past, they now are doing whatever it takes to keep your business through valuable customer services.

    If you are using a personal finance software program for managing your budget, generally there will be a whole section in the program devoted to helping you connect with your bank. With this bank connection, you will be able to regularly download the information from your bank to the software on your computer, so you can update your current financial records.

2. Companies directly. You can go directly to the credit card or utility company's website to sign up for their bill payment service. Essentially, you are giving permission to both the company and your bank to exchange the necessary financial information. Then, what the company will do, when you give the go-ahead, is electronically go to your bank and get the payment from your account.

    The terminology on the websites can sometimes be confusing initially. The text on the credit card company website may say it will *make a payment,* which means the company will go to your bank and electronically *extract the payment* from your account. One advantage of signing up with the individual company websites is the ability to view your complete bill and transaction history and monitor your current activity.

3. Aggregation services. Aggregation companies offer their own independent online services, including bill payment, directly to customers who do not have account aggregation services through their online bank or other financial institutions. Their service will gather ("aggregate") and link all the various websites where you have online account information, such as your bank, credit card companies, utilities, mortgage company, investments, and 401(k) account, and make them all conveniently available on one secure website.

    Using a bill payment service with an aggregation service makes it convenient for you to pay all your bills from one website and have access to all your other financial records. Some account aggregation companies also offer the additional service of tracking your spending so you can view your spending history—this again is *after the fact.*

Many of these online programs offer free 30-day trials and then may charge a monthly, quarterly, or annual subscription fee. Depending on your personal online comfort and style, time constraints, how much you take advantage of all the options available, as well as your actual budget, these services can be worth the fees. Be sure to weigh all the advantages, disadvantages, and what you actually get for your money when making the decision to sign up.

To sign up for an aggregation service, you will need to create your own account, which will require a user name (or user ID) and a password. See "Selecting Passwords" for more information about setting up a password. When you log on to that service with your new user name and password, you are then able to go to the section within the site where you can view your different accounts and portfolios and manage transactions as if you were actually on that website directly. This service eliminates going back and forth to multiple websites and entering different user names and passwords for each of your different accounts.

Some examples of aggregation services that offer an online budget service are Mvelopes® Personal (*www.moneytracker.mvelopes.com*), Microsoft Money (*www.microsoft.com/money/default.mspx*), and Quicken Personal Products (*quicken.intuit.com/personal-finance*). The last two are available as software packages and offer online services. Mvelopes® Personal is a dedicated online home budgeting system.

Cost of Services for Online Bill Payment. By now, you are probably wondering how much these services are going to cost you. Monthly or transaction fees for these services vary from free to nominal, costing approximately $5 to $15 per month, depending on the number of transactions as well as the competitive nature of the industry at the time. Some services will limit or charge by the number of bills you pay each month. However, now there is enough competition in the industry, making it easier to find banks or services with very low or no fees.

Getting Set Up for Online Bill Payment. Whatever option you use, you will need to initially go to the various websites and sign up (or "register") for their service. Usually, there will be a tab, button, or box that says "register," "sign up," or "log in" to get you started.

Before you do this, be sure to gather up your bills and bank statements, so you have your account numbers, addresses, phone numbers, and amounts available ahead of time. Also, be thinking about what user ID (also called user name) and password you want to use. See the "Selecting Passwords" box for more detailed information.

When you get to the website, start off with a patient approach and be prepared initially to spend time reading and understanding the directions and filling in a lot of detailed information. Depending on how user-friendly the sites are, you will be prompted through the setup process with helpful instructions, numbers that let you know how many more steps left to go, and how to get more help.

SELECTING PASSWORDS

Pick a user ID name and password that will be easy for you to remember for each website service. The more you are online and using different websites, the more information you will have to manage. Be sure your password is safe by picking a word or set of characters that no one else could figure out. This means avoiding passwords that are traceable, like names, birth dates, addresses, phone numbers, Social Security numbers, or simple sequences (like 12345 or abcdef). Many websites will give you their required criteria for passwords, such as minimum number of characters to use, combination of numbers and letters, and "case sensitive," or always use the same lowercase and uppercase letter each time you log on. Some suggestions for passwords are your pet's birthday, your engagement date, or short phrases meaningful to you ("my99fordisred" or "good4u"). To be on the safe side, change your passwords every 90 days.

Password hint: When you initially set up your password, you will usually be asked a question and answer to use for a password hint in the event you forget your password and need help. Some companies use this approach to help you remember your actual password. Other companies use this approach to verify that you are who you say you are. When you forget your password, you will need to answer the password hint question. An answer will arrive by email, which will either simply give you your password or set you up with a different password, which you can later change.

See the "Online Information Record" section on page 25 for a place to record all your different passwords.

In some situations, when you are not ready with all the details and take extra long to fill in requested information, you could be "timed out." This means the website automatically logs you out, and often you will lose the information you just entered. I know that frustration very well, so I encourage you to have all the details handy and an extra dose of patience when you are just getting started.

Sometime before you complete the setup process, you will be asked if you agree to the terms and conditions. By clicking the "I Agree" or "I Accept" button, you are "signing" the document electronically, just as if you physically signed a paper document and mailed it to the company.

Once you have completed all the steps, you will receive a confirmation by email letting you know you can go to the website, log in with your new user name and password, and start using their services.

Take your time and learn how all of these steps work and, eventually, your comfort level will increase tremendously every time you go online to use the service.

Will My Money Be Safe if I Bank Online?

Worrying about having all of your personal financial information exposed on the Internet is not unfounded. Established banks and companies have been well aware of the potential danger. Consequently, due to the enormous need for security when dealing with this level of personal financial information, these businesses use the highest level of security currently available in the industry. Read through the security information thoroughly on your bank's website and any other websites where you store financial information to learn how they handle security.

These financial institutions want to make sure they are providing a secure site for you while you are visiting and using their websites. You will often see text on Internet sites that states your account information and transactions are being protected by encryption using SSL (Secure Sockets Layer) technology. Basically, when your account information is passing back and forth between two different secure websites, or your computer and a secure website, encryption is a technology that totally scrambles every bit of information, so it is impossible to decipher during the transmission time. It's a little like our Navajo "code talkers" during WWII who spoke in Navajo as they passed the highest security information back and forth and who could not be understood by *any* other country.

Encryption prevents any party from intercepting the information and prevents eavesdropping, tampering, or forged messages while the information is not yet secured inside a protected website.

Another way websites provide more security and help protect your privacy while you are using their services is to log you out of the online banking service after ten minutes of inactivity. This is a very safe precaution. It also can be a frustrating one, if you are in the middle of setting up a transaction and suddenly need to dig through some files to find a specific detail, only to return and notice you have been logged out and all the previous work you put in erased. A good habit to establish on your own when finished on a website is to *log off as soon as you have completed working on your accounts.*

Privacy Issues

You may be asking, What about identity theft? Again, your fears are valid. Identity theft happens when someone gains access to and uses your personal information, such as your name, drivers license, Social Security number, birth date, credit card number, or other identifying information, without your permission to make purchases or to commit fraud or other crimes. This is another reason you want to be very careful when setting up user names and passwords. Be especially careful about keeping this information private and in a safe place.

Protecting your financial records is enormously important for preserving your privacy. *Monitor your online records and reports regularly to be sure you recognize all the transactions.* At the same time, remember that your regular mail is still intensely sought after by mail thieves, so check your financial bank and credit card statements often to notice any mail tampering.

You also can take an active part in preventing fraud by periodically reviewing your credit rating. See the "Credit Bureaus and Identity Theft Hotline" section. These credit bureaus will provide you with a credit report for a small fee. If you have very specific reasons to be concerned, you may want to sign up for their email notification systems, which alert consumers whenever their credit profiles change. The annual fee may seem pricey, but if the information prevents a theft attempt, it is well worth it.

Opt-out Option. One last note on privacy. Remember to watch for Opt-out choices in the literature or online when you are setting up your service with any company, including your financial institution, phone, utility, and credit card companies. Opt-out means you are opting out of receiving any information or direct marketing materials unrelated to your account from that company itself. They will also assure you that your information is not being shared with any outside companies. Be sure to fill out the necessary paperwork or make the phone call to initiate this choice. This is your responsibility.

Opt Out Resources

Use these resources for getting your name off of lists like direct marketing, telemarketing, email lists, credit bureaus, lenders, and many more.

- 888-5-OPT-OUT (888-567-8688)
- www.ftc.gov/privacy/protect.shtm
- www.dmaconsumers.org
- www.optoutprescreen.com
- 101-creditreport.com/optout.htm
- www.privacyrights.org/letters/letters.htm
- www.donotcall.gov or (1-888-382-1222)*

*The National Do Not Call Registry is managed by the Federal Trade Commission (FTC), the nation's consumer protection agency. It is enforced by the FTC, the Federal Communications Commission (FCC), and state law enforcement officials.

Credit Reports and Fico Scores

Your credit score now has a more significant impact on your financial life than ever before. A low score could be costing you hundreds of dollars on your mortgage, car payment, and credit cards. It can also impact rates for your health and car insurance as well as interfere with your search for employment and a place to rent.

Take advantage of the free annual credit reports available from all three agencies by staggering these requests throughout the year. Watch for any errors or suspicious activity showing up on your credit reports and report these immediately.

There are numerous sources for more thorough information regarding your credit report available online, in the library, and through other books.

Stay current with this information. The guidelines on how your credit score is affected have been changing a great deal over the last few years. With the ongoing rapid changes in the financial world you can no longer depend on the accuracy of information you may have learned years ago.

Remember that one of the best and basic ways to gradually improve your score and keep your score high is to make all your payments *on time* and *in full*.

To order your free credit report and get more information, visit *www. annualcreditreport.com* or call 877-322-8228 or write to Credit Report Request Service, P.O. Box 105281, Atlanta, GA 30348-5281.

Credit Bureaus and Identity Theft Hotline

The current three credit bureaus as of this printing are:

1. Experian: 888-397-3742, *www.experian.com*
2. Equifax: 800-685-1111, *www.equifax.com*
3. TransUnion: 800-916-8800, *www.transunion.com*

Fico Score Calculations

Know the basics of what impacts your score the most.

35%–Payment History
Late payments, including payments below the minimum requirement, have a huge hit on your score. The more recent the late payment, the lower the score on your report.

30%–Outstanding Debt
This evaluates how close you are to the credit limit on any account. Keep smaller balances spread out over more cards, rather than maxing out one card by consolidating all debt on that card.

15%–Credit History
Do not close old cards if you've had them for many years and they show a long history for you, even if you have not had any activity on that card for awhile— especially if you do not have many other cards showing any credit history. Closing cards used to be the advice in the past, but this is no longer the case. The object is to show a long established history of credit and timely payments.

10%–Type of Credit
This evaluates the mix of credit, including installment loans, mortgages, leases, credit cards, etc. Finance company credit is one of the most negative.

10%–Inquiries
Every inquiry by credit promotions, employers, credit card applications, bank reviews, etc. shows up on your credit report. Be aware that not all inquiries are treated the same.

TOP 12 LIST OF HOW TO PROTECT YOURSELF FROM FRAUD AND IDENTITY THEFT

1. Avoid ever giving out your entire Social Security Number (SSN), the last four digits of your SSN, your birth date, your mother's maiden name, any financial account numbers, credit card 3-digit verification number, or your password by phone, in the mail, or online if you did not initiate the contact, do not know the caller, or did not type in the website address.

2. Stay suspicious with calls sounding professional and helpful from financial-related companies or "Security and Fraud Departments." If they verify much of your personal information and only need you to provide information on 1 or 2 items, do not give out this information. Call this company back on a number you already have or look them up (statements, phone book, Internet) and then verify if this call was valid.

3. Stay alert for "Phishing" (an email fraud scam where the message looks like it came from a legitimate and trustworthy bank, business, or online organization asking for your personal and financial information for various purposes). Never click on hyperlinks or cut and paste these links in any suspicious or unknown emails. Go directly to the website instead and log into your account.

4. If you do give out any critical personal information, or have your wallet, checkbook, or credit cards stolen, file a police report right away.

5. Pay attention to late or missing bills and any credit cards you never applied for. Follow up immediately.

6. Collect your mail right away. Do not let mail received or outgoing mail sit in an unsecured mailbox.

7. Do not carry your social security card, passport, or multiple credit cards on you when not needed.

8. If you are still using checks and order new ones, pick them up at the bank. Do NOT have them mailed to your home.

9. Shred all credit card offers and all other financial papers showing any of your personal and account number information.

10. Before you dispose of your computer, delete all stored personal information. Do an online "wipe programs" search to find this software. Use this program to destroy your data and delete your files on your hard drive.

11. If you find out someone did steal your social security number, contact one of the three consumer credit reporting agencies listed and place an initial fraud alert on your credit reports right away.

12. Continue to monitor your credit reports and statements. Watch for any new fraudulent accounts. Some thieves will wait months until you feel safe again before using your information.

If you feel you may be a victim of identity theft, contact the Federal Trade Commission's Identity Theft Hotline toll-free at 1-877-ID-THEFT (1-877-438-4338) or visit the U.S. government's central website for information about identity theft at *www.ftc.gov/idtheft*.

Online Resources—Identity Theft

- Federal Trade Commission–ID Theft
  www.consumer.gov/idtheft/id_laws.htm
- OnGuard Online–Identity Theft
  onguardonline.gov/idtheft.html
- FCIC: Preventing Identity Theft: A Guide for Consumers
  www.pueblo.gsa.gov/cic_text/money/preventidtheft/preventing.htm
- AARP–Preventing Identity Theft
  www.aarp.org/learntech/personal_finance/identity_theft_intro.html
- 101 Identity Theft–Pre-Approved Offers in the Mail and Identity Theft
  101-identitytheft.com/bulkmail.htm
- 101 Identity Theft–Prevention and Victim Information
  101-identitytheft.com
- Your Credit Advisor–The Ultimate Guide to Identity Theft Prevention
  www.yourcreditadvisor.com/blog/2006/10/the_ultimate_gu.html

Summary of Advantages and Disadvantages of Online Banking and Paying Bills Online

Advantages

Less Paper, More convenience. If you ever stressed over a misplaced bill because of that pile of unmanaged mail, the idea of less paper and more convenient payments will come as a major relief. With online bill payments, you can select a payment method of "recurring payments" for ongoing bills like rent, car payments, etc., that automatically repeat the same payment each month.

One-time and periodic payments can be set up months in advance. No more saving paper bills in special folders to remember six months down the road. You also can list the exact date you want your payment to go out—the number of days in advance of the due date (five business days is generally recommended) or on payday or any other date.

Many companies will continue to mail your paper bills for review, sometimes with a small fee if you prefer to save these records.

Anywhere, Anytime. Once you have access to the Internet, no matter where you are, you can view statement activity; confirm the balance, finance charge, and due dates; pay bills; and transfer funds every hour of every day. Suddenly, your financial life can revolve around *your* personal schedule instead of the 9 to 5 schedule of most banks and businesses. Transferring funds at 2 AM while in your bathrobe is now an option.

Staying on top of your finances while you are traveling, whether business or personal, is no longer an issue. Many hotels offer Internet access, public libraries offer free Internet access, and Internet cafes exist in many cities around the world. This means no more bills to catch up on when you return.

Save Time, Save Money. Countless hours annually can be saved when you are no longer buying stamps, finding bill-paying supplies, writing checks, and stuffing envelopes. Tax-prep time and cost also may be reduced with many of your records in one place.

Obviously, you will be buying fewer stamps, which could pay for a few lunches a year. Add to that the savings of the annual cost of purchasing 150 or more checks; your supply of checks will last for years. Don't forget to factor in the value of your time. And finally, consider the saved late fees of $25 to $35 that will be avoided as each monthly bill is paid automatically on time.

Count on Security and Privacy. Always watch for the little icons (usually yellow) that look like padlocks, usually located on the status bar on the website. If you look to the right of the address bar in Microsoft Explorer, you will see the padlock icon. Click your mouse on this icon. Information will show up to explain the level of security being used. You can also watch for a website URL that begins with "https." The "s" stands for secure.

Peace of Mind. Now you can focus your time and energy on more significant people and events in your life and not have to face the draining monthly ritual of paying bills. Another payoff is the excellent credit history you establish by paying bills regularly and on time. And finally, if you worry about losing your financial records, rest assured large financial websites are well equipped to back up financial information regularly. Since these are your financial records, be on the safe side and *always* back up your own records on a regular basis.

Disadvantages

Downtime of the Website. There are going to be times when the system is down due to a power outage or no connection, or the site itself may be down temporarily for servicing or updating. It may happen on the weekend or late evening when you want to get online the most. If your financial situation is urgent, there is always the standby of the telephone. Some of the banks and credit card companies have 24-hour service. Choose a reliable bill pay system where downtime is minimal.

Downtime for your Computer. Who has not had problems with their computer, connection, or some other technical issue? This downtime may be more challenging for you if you also have opted for the paperless route and have no paper records or printouts to refer to in an emergency when you really need to get online. Be sure to back up your electronic files by saving them on CDs, or other backup systems regularly for this same reason. Even though financial websites back up their information, you probably have a great deal of other financial information you want safely saved on your own back up system.

Also, until the paperless system is perfected, it is a good idea to hold on to a majority of your paper financial records.

Time Investment. Getting set up online will take a little time in the beginning as you register and enter all your information. Learning how each site works and exploring all of your options can take more time, depending on how new you are to this process and how the banking or other sites are set up. In the beginning as you are getting more familiar with online banking, it may take a while to get comfortable with each bill-pay transaction. You may find yourself going online and checking frequently to make sure the transaction went through correctly.

Fees. Depending on the services you have signed up for, there generally will be some monthly fees involved. But, considering the savings of your time, energy, and peace of mind, the fee may be a small price to pay for the convenience of having all your bills handled online.

Lost Float Time

In the past, it was common to calculate in a few extra days of float time after sending a check, before it would be cashed and actually hit your bank. Now with debit cards and online bill pay, the day you debit or the date you set up your bill pay transaction is the day the money is withdrawn from your account. Bye-bye float time. Keep this in mind especially when operating with a joint account. There may be times when your partner arranges to pay a lot of bills and your account balance gets very low. These are the times you want to be sure to maintain communication with your partner before using your joint account to make a number of spontaneous, unplanned debits.

How does *The Budget Kit* Fit in with this Cashless Society?

Using any of the numerous personal finance software packages certainly can help you balance your checkbook, track your checking and savings accounts as well as your investments, pinpoint records you will need for taxes, and print out overflowing reports in every chart, graph, and style you can imagine. Armed with all this information, you may feel like you are taking charge and feel totally in control, which you absolutely can be with such functional and powerful tools.

However, if you are noticing that your spending habits have not changed, your debt load has not come down, and you are still frustrated and not clear about your total financial picture, it may be time for a closer, hands-on review of the situation. Go back through *The Budget Kit* sections, especially Part Two, and note any worksheets you previously used manually but are no longer using because of your new software program.

The bottom line when it comes to managing your money, whether manually or online, is still to have an effective, organized plan or system that you totally understand that gives you a comprehensive monthly and yearly financial picture. You want this picture to be realistic and based on accurate tracking and records (of all cash, checks, cashless transactions, and associated fees), so you know exactly where you stand financially at any time. You then can see immediately what adjustments, if any, you need to make to stay on course and within your budget guidelines.

The Budget Kit explains the basic concepts and steps in a simple, user-friendly format and gives you all the easy tools and worksheets you need for manually accomplishing all of these steps. Understanding these concepts is a critical first step before transferring over to *any* personal finance software or online system for peak efficiency and effectiveness.

As more and more new cashless methods of spending emerge, and less physical contact is made with cash, it is easier to become further removed and out of touch with the reality of your financial situation. Having an understanding of the basic concepts and some kind of hands-on system in place, like *The Budget Kit,* keeps you in closer contact with your money and helps you better adjust to and track all the new technical and financial changes, charges, and records being introduced.

What About the "Dual" Household?

These past few years I have noticed more couples who were getting stuck with their "method of choice" when it came to going electronic or staying manual. Each was stubbornly holding on to their method of choice and just as stubbornly resisting the method used by their partner. What to do? The best solution for my clients has been to use *BOTH!*

Once you no longer are putting energy into defending why your method is better, you each can focus on getting the budget done. It may seem a bit redundant, but in the end, each partner is involved in his/her own way and they are taking more time to communicate and collaborate so his/her numbers and records are accurate. The ultimate goal of getting a handle on spending, getting out of debt, and saving more money is eventually accomplished—and with less friction.

In many cases, one of the transition options was to have one partner use the Excel version of *The Budget Kit* primary worksheets (*moneytracker.com/ books-TheBudgetKitExcel.htm*) so they could still feel they were on the computer, and the other partner entered information into this workbook.

My final motto always is "If it works, stay with it." You'll know when and if you are ready to change systems.

Online Information Record

Keeping track of all the different information you need to log on to secure Internet sites can be daunting. If you haven't already come up with some system for keeping all those personal user names and passwords in one place, use this **Online Information Record** to gather your information together.

A word of caution: If you are using online banking and other online financial services and have most of your financial records stored online, be extremely careful to keep your password and PIN information private. Your PIN confirms your identity and unlocks the access to your accounts. Decide if your spouse or children will have access to this information. Do not give this information to anyone or leave it where someone can easily see it or find it. Protect your PIN and password as carefully as you would your ATM PIN.

As an extra precaution, periodically change your password and PIN number.

After you fill out this form, it is a good idea to tear out these pages and keep them in a very secure place.

ONLINE INFORMATION RECORD

WEBSITE NAME AND WEB ADDRESS	USER NAME/ID	PASSWORD	PIN/OTHER #

ACCOUNT	PASSWORD HINT—Q/A	CUSTOMER/TECH SUPPORT #	NOTES

One longtime reader wrote to say: "When I started keeping records it was like an awakening. In seven years I saved $100,000 thanks to your book. By the end of this year, which will be just over nine years, that number should be close to a quarter of a million." It's amazing how the numbers start to accelerate after a certain point.

This reader was exceptionally disciplined and motivated. Whenever he did not spend money (e.g., walk versus taxi, video versus movie, library versus bookstore), he would actually put that savings aside and record it in his book. On last conversation he still continues to feel no deprivation. He now *knows* he can buy anything he wants, and is very satisfied with how he chooses to spend his money.

As you fill in the following pages in Part One, you will see more clearly what you already have and what you still would like to have.

Writing down what you want in black and white is always a powerful way of becoming more focused and motivated in your daily living. Part Two will give you the tools for accomplishing your goals.

- **Net Worth Statement**
- **Identified Goals Worksheet**
- **Goals Savings Record**
- **Needs/Wants List**

Net Worth Statement

An important step in gaining financial control is to take an accounting of what your total financial worth is. Every year, your net worth should be tabulated to enable you to review your progress and compare it with your financial goals. In addition, a Net Worth Statement is a valuable aid in planning your estate and establishing a record for loan and insurance purposes.

On the following **Net Worth Statement** worksheet, total up all your "Assets" (what you **OWN**). Next, total up all our "Liabilities" (what you **OWE**). Subtract the amount of the "Liabitities" total from the "Assets" total to calculate your "Total Net Worth."

Your goal is to have a positive Net Worth that increases each year.

NET WORTH STATEMENT

DATE COMPLETED _____

ASSETS—WHAT YOU OWN	Amount
Cash: On Hand	_____
Checking Accounts	_____
Savings Accounts	_____
Money Markets	_____
Other	_____
Real Estate/Property:	
Principal Residence	_____
Second Residence	_____
Land	_____
Income Property	_____
Other (Business, partnerships, etc.)	_____
Investments: (Market Value)	
Cash Value Life Insurance	_____
Certificates of Deposit	_____
U.S. Treasury Bills/Savings Bonds	_____
Stocks	_____
Bonds	_____
Mutual Funds	_____
Limited Partnerships	_____
Annuities	_____
IRA–Regular/Roth/Keogh Plan	_____
401(k), 403(b), or 457 Plans	_____
Pension Plan/Retirement Plans	_____
Other (Stock options, bonuses, etc.)	_____
Personal Loans Receivable	_____
Personal Property: (Present Value)	
Cars, Trucks, Vehicles	_____
Recreational Vehicle/Boat	_____
Electronic Equipment	_____
Home Furnishings	_____
Home Entertainment Equipment	_____
Appliances and Furniture	_____
Collectibles/Antiques	_____
Jewelry and Furs	_____
Other	_____

LIABILITIES—WHAT YOU OWE	Amount
Current Debts:	_____
Household	_____
Medical	_____
Credit Cards	_____
Department Store Cards	_____
Back Taxes (Federal, State, Property)	_____
Legal	_____
Child Support	_____
Alimony	_____
Other	_____
Mortgages:	
Principal Residence	_____
Second Residence	_____
Land	_____
Income Property	_____
Other	_____
Loans:	
Home Equity	_____
Bank/Finance Company	_____
Bank/Finance Company	_____
Automobiles, Vehicles	_____
Recreational Vehicle/Boat	_____
Education/Student	_____
Life Insurance	_____
Personal (from family or friends)	_____
Retirement Accounts	_____
Other	_____
	_____
	_____
	_____

Total Assets	

Total Assets minus Total Liabilities = **Net Worth**

Total Liabilities	

Total Net Worth $ _____

Setting Financial Goals

Jan was never successful at saving even though she made a great income as a loan officer. Once she started tracking her spending and learned how to work out a budget, it made a "million percent" difference in her life. She created a savings account to buy a house, which she never could do before. She practiced the "pay yourself first" technique, considered her savings as a bill, and successfully saved $15,000 in one year and bought her house. Now she's even more motivated about saving and is planning to invest in additional real estate."

Setting financial goals is one of the most important steps for gaining financial control. When you have a goal, you have the motivation needed to follow a money-management plan.

The worksheets on the following pages will help you identify and record your financial goals and develop a plan for reaching them.

To begin, ask yourself what is important to you. What will make you happy and/or be a significant accomplishment? Define your goals in specific attainable terms (such as buying a red two-door BMW instead of just buying a new car) and write them down. You then have taken the first step toward reaching your goals.

You can find more goal-setting information with a search on Amazon or Google.

Immediate/Short-Range Goals

These goals are any that you have identified for the next month and/or year. Your goals depend on your interests and your lifestyle. Perhaps you want to save your Christmas money in advance this year, buy a digital camera, or pay off a major debt.

Do not forget your emergency fund. If you do not have at least three months' take-home pay set aside as a protection against unforeseen problems or disasters, this should be your *number-one goal*. Once you have the security of knowing you are covered for possible emergencies, you can comfortably focus on your other goals.

When you reach the goals you have identified in this section, you will have more confidence and discipline for the more aggressive goals in the Middle- and Long-Range Goals section.

Middle and Long-Range Goals

Middle-range goals are those you hope to reach two to five years from now. Maybe you are dreaming of a new home, thinking of starting a family, or planning a trip abroad.

Long-range goals include plans beyond five years, including college tuition and retirement. By thinking about longer-range periods, you will make wiser use of your money. With time on your side, small amounts of money saved regularly for 10 to 40 years will grow tremendously. And if you pay closer attention to where you invest your money, it will grow even more.

Family Affair

If you have a family, bring everyone together to discuss their interests and goals. Children need to take part in this activity not only to give their input, but to learn from the process for their own adult years.

There seldom is enough money to reach everyone's goals. When Dad wants the latest HDTV, Mom wants a new refrigerator, and your teen wants the latest videophone, compromise is necessary. Each member of the family learns to give and take and decide what is agreeable as a compromise. Rather than drop a major goal altogether, try extending the deadline date.

One family decided to cut back and save for a car. In two-and-a-half-years' time this family of four with two young children saved $18,000. They did not consider it depriving when they chose to cut back on clothing and eating out and did a lot more buying at garage sales and auctions. Each month they also invested $300 without exception in a mutual fund as a dollar cost average approach. The best part was feeling confident in their ability to actually pull it off.

Filling in Your Identified Goals Worksheet

Once you have defined your goals and have written them down under "Goals" on the **Identified Goals Worksheet**, fill in the remainder of the worksheet. Number the "Priority" of each goal listed. Which goal do you want first, second, and so on? Which can wait a few months or another year?

What is your "Target Date"? Six months, one year, six years? Every goal should have a beginning and an ending date. Once you have committed yourself to a time frame in your mind and on paper, you have taken one more positive step toward reaching your goal.

"Cost Estimate" helps develop your estimating ability and forces you to do some research. By calling, reading, or shopping to determine the estimated cost of buying a computer or putting in a pool, for example, your goal becomes more than just a dream.

If you have money in savings, how much of that "Amount Already Saved" do you want to use toward your goal? Write it down. Commit yourself to an amount.

"How to Achieve" is crucial. What are you willing to do to make your goal a reality? Will it involve working overtime or finding a second job? Will it mean tradeoffs—cutting back or eliminating expenses such as movies, meals out, or smoking—so you can reach your goal?

How much will you have to save each week, month, or year to reach your goals? If you have a difficult time setting aside money for your goals, arrange with your bank for direct deposit from your paycheck.

The **Goals Savings Record** on *Page 37* is a great place for keeping track of your savings for your goals. Take your "Cost Estimate" figure from the **Identified Goals Worksheet** and write it in the space next to "Total Cost." Divide that figure by 12 to see how much money you need to save every month. Each month, record your savings and balance. You will be excited to actually see yourself coming closer to your goal.

Pay Attention to Your Money

If you have a strong desire to reach your goal and you *really* want your money to work for you, you must pay attention to what you do with your money.

Earlier, I mentioned having time on your side and paying closer attention to your money. For long-range goals (college, early retirement) where large amounts are necessary, these two factors are critical.

Let's say that you decide to save $100 at the beginning of every month for ten years to reach your goal. You could stash that money under your favorite mattress and have $12,000 at the end of ten years. Obviously, that method is not the wisest or safest.

If you had chosen to take that monthly $100 to your bank and let it sit safely in a savings account and draw 3 to 5 percent compounded daily interest, after ten years you would have made nearly $2,000 to $3,500 "free" dollars for doing nothing more than driving to your local bank or transferring online. In the meantime, you would have saved $15,536.81 for your goal.

On the other hand, if you were to take time to find an account that pays 10 percent compounded daily interest for that same $100 every month for ten years, your reward for your research time would be an extra $4,995.61 over the 5 percent interest from the bank, or an extra $8,532.42 over the mattress investment, giving you $20,532.42 for your goal!

Saving $100 a Month for Ten Years

	Under the Mattress	*3–5% Interest*	*10% Interest*
Total Saved	$12,000	$15,536.81	$20,532.42

These figures do exclude the inflation factor; however, the more years you have to invest and the higher interest rate or return amount you get, the more money you will make. Read financial books, newspapers, and magazines, surf the Web, or talk to your financial planner, broker, accountant, or local banker to examine your options. *When you learn how to effectively invest your hard-earned money, you can be confident that you will reach your goals.*

IDENTIFIED GOALS WORKSHEET

IMMEDIATE/SHORT-RANGE GOALS

Priority	Goal	Target Date	Cost Estimate	Amount Already Saved	How to Achieve (Amount per month, second job, etc.)

MIDDLE- AND LONG-RANGE GOALS

Priority	Goal	Target Date	Cost Estimate	Amount Already Saved	How to Achieve (Amount per month, second job, etc.)

GOALS SAVINGS RECORD

Goal: Roth IRA													Total Cost: 3,500
	JAN.	FEB.	MAR.	APR.	MAY	JUNE	JULY	AUG.	SEPT.	OCT.	NOV.	DEC.	
Deposit	292	292	250	275	350	292	270	320	292	292	290	285	Monthly Deposit: 292
Balance	292	584	834	1,109	1,459	1,751	2,021	2,341	2,633	2,925	3,215	3,500	**Total:** 3,500

Goal:													Total Cost:
	JAN.	FEB.	MAR.	APR.	MAY	JUNE	JULY	AUG.	SEPT.	OCT.	NOV.	DEC.	
Deposit													Monthly Deposit:
Balance													**Total:**

Goal:													Total Cost:
	JAN.	FEB.	MAR.	APR.	MAY	JUNE	JULY	AUG.	SEPT.	OCT.	NOV.	DEC.	
Deposit													Monthly Deposit:
Balance													**Total:**

Goal:													Total Cost:
	JAN.	FEB.	MAR.	APR.	MAY	JUNE	JULY	AUG.	SEPT.	OCT.	NOV.	DEC.	
Deposit													Monthly Deposit:
Balance													**Total:**

Goal:													Total Cost:
	JAN.	FEB.	MAR.	APR.	MAY	JUNE	JULY	AUG.	SEPT.	OCT.	NOV.	DEC.	
Deposit													Monthly Deposit:
Balance													**Total:**

Goal:													Total Cost:
	JAN.	FEB.	MAR.	APR.	MAY	JUNE	JULY	AUG.	SEPT.	OCT.	NOV.	DEC.	
Deposit													Monthly Deposit:
Balance													**Total:**

Goal:													Total Cost:
	JAN.	FEB.	MAR.	APR.	MAY	JUNE	JULY	AUG.	SEPT.	OCT.	NOV.	DEC.	
Deposit													Monthly Deposit:
Balance													**Total:**

Goal:													Total Cost:
	JAN.	FEB.	MAR.	APR.	MAY	JUNE	JULY	AUG.	SEPT.	OCT.	NOV.	DEC.	
Deposit													Monthly Deposit:
Balance													**Total:**

Goal:													Total Cost:
	JAN.	FEB.	MAR.	APR.	MAY	JUNE	JULY	AUG.	SEPT.	OCT.	NOV.	DEC.	
Deposit													Monthly Deposit:
Balance													**Total:**

The formula for determining the monthly amount to save for each of your goals is:

Total cost of your goal ÷ Number of months left to date needed = Amount per month you need to save.

Needs/Wants List

Taking Further Control of Finances

This Needs/Wants List is like a "wish list" that helps you take financial control one step further. This section is designed to be a guideline for those times when you have extra money but want to be sure that you wisely use your money on priority items versus impulse items.

Needs and Wants Versus Goals

Needs, wants, and goals as used in this workbook are all the things that you would like to have but must wait until all your required needs are handled first. With your improved budgeting skills and money awareness, you know you will have the capability to eventually acquire these items.

The difference between needs and wants and goals is primarily in the cost and the significance of the desired items. Goals are more significant plans involving time and the gradual accumulation of funds for major purchases, such as a home theater system, car, or home. Elimination of a major debt is also a goal.

Needs and wants, on the other hand, are the smaller-ticket items. These are the purchases made when extra money (known as discretionary money) is left over after paying the bills and putting aside money for your savings and your goals.

How to Use this List

Throughout the year, you probably see or think about many things you need or would like to have, but don't have the extra cash at the time to buy them. Jot down all your ideas on this Needs/Wants List.

Items on your list can range from things seen on websites, in mail-order catalogs, TV advertisements, or stores to activities such as the opera, a concert, or a ski weekend. Having these ideas written down also will make it easier for you to remember to watch for sales and list gift ideas as they come up.

At the same time, make a check mark either under the "Need" (necessities for your everyday well-being, such as food, housing, or medicine) or "Want" (which are nice to have, such as a DVD player for the car, jewelry, or theater tickets, but which you can do without if you have to) column. This way, you can make sure you take care of needs first when extra money is available. Record the source and cost of your items. When you are ready to purchase the listed item, the necessary information will be handy.

By using this Needs/Wants List, you start establishing priorities and identifying what you really do want when you have extra money. When you have an extra $50 (which you determine after completing your Monthly Budget Worksheet in Part Two) and a sale suddenly catches your eye, you won't be so apt to impulsively buy something. It will be easier to remember when extra money is available that there was something else you really wanted or needed more.

A Family Affair

The ability to prioritize is a valuable skill for all age levels. If your children ask for something when money is tight, write down their wishes on the list or have the children write them down. Your action assures your children that you are *acknowledging* their needs and wants rather than saying that they just can't have something, or that you "can't afford it." Remember that you are constantly being a role model with all of your words and actions. These are all subtle ways of setting the tone and message for how your child may view and handle finances as an adult. In this way, children also learn to establish priorities, make choices, and develop patience along with delayed gratification.

When money does become available, either from your budget or from their gifts or other money sources, your children can choose which item on the list to buy based on cost and priority instead of reacting impulsively to the first temptation that catches their eye in the mall, on TV, or on the Internet.

NEEDS/WANTS LIST

PARENTS

Date	Item	Need	Want	Source (store, catalog, Internet, other)	Cost

CHILDREN

Date	Item	Need	Want	Source (store, catalog, Internet, other)	Cost

"As a student, I used to carry my Budget Kit workbook with me every day in my pack. For anyone not used to figures, this workbook is an easy way to start. When I wrote things down every day it made me think, 'Do I really need this?' 'Where could I save?' 'Is there something I'd rather spend my money on?' Writing everything down and seeing the total picture clearly gave me those answers and a real incentive to change."

Now that you are ready to develop a spending plan (a budget), let me walk you through the process just as if I were sitting with you at your dining room table, as I do with my clients.

The three boldface sections on the right, **Yearly Budget Worksheet (Non-Monthly Anticipated Expenses), Monthly Budget Worksheet,** and **Monthly Expense Record,** form the keystone for the whole budgeting process for all households. The other forms are supplemental worksheets for households with varying financial needs. Over the years as I have worked with clients and talked with readers using this workbook, I have found that using these three sections in this order has provided the most significant results.

For years, readers have had their favorite sections. Some used only one or two sections, where others used nearly all of them. The purpose of this revised workbook is still to give you the same flexibility to pick and choose the sections that will work best for you. However, I want you to have the opportunity to understand the sections early on so you don't overlook one that could be particularly valuable for you.

The **Yearly Budget Worksheet (Non-Monthly Anticipated Expenses)** is the *missing link* worksheet that I have found makes all the difference in the world for people, right from the beginning. By starting with this overall yearly picture of where your money goes above and beyond the regular monthly bills and expenses, you see immediately and graphically why you are usually short each month, why you have so little to show for all the good money you make, or why your debt never seems to go down each year.

The **Monthly Budget Worksheet** is the next critical tool. As you begin each new month, use this worksheet to streamline the whole bill paying and budget planning process. This form helps you to anticipate all the bills as well as the majority of incidental expenses (hair coloring, child's field trip, photo developing, etc.) so you know and can project ahead of time (before the month even begins) how much money you will need for the entire month. You will immediately see if you are going to be short so you have time to start making some arrangements and changes. You also will know what you can and cannot afford in terms of impulsive splurge events.

• Yearly Budget Worksheet (Non-Monthly Anticipated Expenses)

Suggestion List—Additional Non-Monthly Expenses

Gift Giving Worksheet

Christmas/Holiday Expense Worksheet

• Monthly Budget Worksheet

Online Information Record

Variable Income Worksheet

Windfall Planner

Multiple Sales Monthly Planner

Debt Payoff Record

Debt Repayment Worksheet

Credit Card Purchase Record

• Monthly Expense Record

Summary-for-the-Year Record

The **Monthly Expense Record** is the final and most important tool that lets you know where all your money has *really gone* for the whole month. This is your reality check on what your spending habits (like the coffee and bagel, CDs and books, etc.) are actually costing you.

These three core worksheets are available on excel and look exactly like the worksheets in this section. They are available at *http://moneytracker.com/ books-TheBudgetKitExcel.htm.*

"I would be lost without my workbook. It's my bible. By keeping it next to the coffee and kids' money for school, the workbook is always handy. I color-code expenses for my kids and under pets I highlight the expenses of the horses in yellow and dogs in red so I know the real cost of each."

Yearly Budget Worksheet
(Non-Monthly Anticipated Expenses)

Why a Yearly Budget Worksheet?

This worksheet is designed to give you a general yearly overview of your *irregular, occasional, non-monthly,* and *periodic* expenses at a glance. This method often provides a more manageable approach than the use of files, notes on the calendar, or even some software programs.

Having this information can prevent those pay periods when you finally have all the bills paid and give a sigh of relief only to be deluged the next day with quarterly HOA dues or property tax bills you had overlooked or not anticipated, which put your whole budget in a tailspin once again.

By having all this information *written down* as early in the year as possible, you can use it to make necessary arrangements ahead of time. How much money should you put aside in your reserve savings account for the dental work, could you postpone that new sofa, how can the vacation be less costly, is it time to cut back on the gifts? By thinking these options through ahead of time and taking action, you won't be falling back on the credit cards or loans to get you through the year.

Filling in Your Yearly Budget Worksheet

Be patient as you go through this first form. It will require more time initially. However, the insights and information you gain will be well worth your time. Once this worksheet is completed, it becomes a valuable reference page for the remainder of the year.

To get started, grab your pencil, eraser, and calculator. Then gather up your checkbook registers or bank statements, insurance papers, credit card statements, and any other related household papers that may give the exact or estimated *amounts* of expenses plus the *months* these expenses are due or paid.

Start at the top left on *page 53*. Look at the expense category and, if it applies to you, move across the page to the right and fill in the exact or estimated amount under the month or months the expense is due. I suggest pencil because as you work this through, changes and new additions will definitely come up.

See the **Suggestion List** at the end of these instructions to find additional and often overlooked expenses that may apply to your household but are not on this worksheet. The worksheet is deliberately kept generic so you can adjust it to your own unique needs.

For those expense categories where you really don't have a clue what the cost will be, guess. That's right. It is okay not to be perfect and it is also more valuable to keep moving through this exercise than to use the missing information as a reason to stop or get discouraged. You are already going through the most important process by thinking about these expenses and filling in most of the information. You can always add to this section later as new or more accurate information becomes available.

Additional Notes About the Categories

This worksheet is a guideline for you. You may find you have to add or cross out and replace certain categories. Remember to do whatever works best for your unique financial picture.

This section will be especially helpful if you are on a very tight budget this year. Some of your expenses like insurance or taxes will be fixed and there will be no room for negotiating or eliminating this expense.

On the other hand, a number of the expenses may not be so immediate, nor be considered "needs," but are still preferred when the extra money is available. When you have the whole picture in front of you and see the total cost, it will be easier to make decisions about how to handle those expenses when the money is still tight.

Be sure to review the **Suggestion List** following these instructions so you can fully take advantage of this worksheet and include all the valuable information that belongs here. Below are a few notes for some of the categories.

Home/yard Maintenance. This can include expenses that range from a new mattress to an addition to the house or backyard. If you have been thinking about new furniture and have been trying to decide when you can afford it, use this **Yearly Budget Worksheet** for your planning.

Auto Expenses. If you stop to think this area through ahead of time, you can estimate when you might need tires or need to take your car in for its 60,000-mile checkup. This also would naturally include regular quarterly oil changes.

Medical Expenses. These are often difficult to know in advance, yet it is helpful to think about the different areas on the **Suggestion List** ahead of time so you can *anticipate* a possible expense rather than *react* to it. Put some estimate down, even the small copays, to remind you of the expenses throughout the year.

Vacations. Plan your vacations in advance. Keep in mind the mini-weekend trip as well as those holiday family visits and summer vacations. Both gifts and vacations are good practice places for learning to live within your income. You may enjoy buying expensive gifts or going on exotic vacations, but if this puts a hardship on your budget, you may have to reevaluate your priorities. Either spend less on these categories or less on some other categories.

Gifts. For some households, these are a minimal expense. Yet for others who place a high priority on gifts, the gift expense area can be a major expense and budget buster when remembering the gifts as well as the party expenses for: Christmas, birthdays, weddings, Mother's and Father's Days, anniversaries, baby showers, graduation, etc. Planning out all this information ahead of time will make it all more manageable.

The **Gift Giving Worksheet** is a separate worksheet to use for outlining all the gifts you plan to give *throughout* the year. You can total the amounts for each month and transfer those totals to the "Gift" category on this worksheet. Even though Christmas gifts are often purchased throughout the year, I do suggest putting the whole Christmas gift expense total under December (unless you know the months you made these early purchases) only to keep this planning simple.

Holiday Events. This expense will vary from household to household depending on how you celebrate Valentine's Day, July 4th, Halloween, Thanksgiving, and other traditional and religious events in your family. Don't forget the cost of decorating the house or purchasing a new Halloween costume along with all the other related expenses. By listing these estimates as well as the others on this page, you will have a more realistic approach to all your upcoming expenses.

The **Christmas/Holiday Expense Worksheet** can help you fine-tune the real expense of the Christmas and holiday season on top of the gift expense. Many of my clients will guess an amount for this category. Then when we work through the details of the real estimate with the worksheet, the total amount is usually three times their guess.

"I started using your book when it got to the point where we just didn't know where all the money was going. I figured most of it was going to meals out, which turned out to be true, but what shocked me was the amount being spent on gifts!"

All of these various expenses are just more examples of "where the money goes."

How to Use this Information

Once you have taken time to estimate and project your upcoming non-monthly expenses, you have valuable information that graphically shows you which months will be light and which ones will be difficult to deal with. At this point you can evaluate each expense and consider your choices: you can cut back, postpone, modify, or eliminate the expense. Which choice best fits your personal needs?

When you total all of these expenses, you can quickly see why there never seems to be enough money. This is where the Reserve Savings Account mentioned earlier in the "How to Use *The Budget Kit*" section now makes more sense. When you total these expenses and divide by 12 (to get your monthly average), you can see how much money must be put aside each month to prepare for these upcoming expenses. You then can transfer this amount onto the **Monthly Budget Worksheet** and list it as Reserve Savings to help you plan ahead for the month.

As you look at this completed worksheet, what does it tell you? First, as mentioned above, you can see which months are going to be high-stress months and which ones will be manageable light months. Now you have a guideline to let you know which month would be better for taking on additional expenses.

Second, you can see what you ideally need to put aside each month to save for all these expenses. If that amount is too much at this time, pick some of the fixed and most expensive categories, like property tax, gifts, auto repairs, etc., and start putting aside one-twelfth of those totals. You also can use the **Goals Saving Record** in Part One or the general **Savings Activity Record** in Part Three to help track your savings.

Third, and most significantly, that monthly average amount is having a major indirect impact on your regular monthly budget, but it's not showing up directly. Consequently, this impact usually shows up in the form of added credit card debt, new home equity line of credit, more or larger loans, financial juggling, doing without, and overall frustration.

Now that you can see this and realize what has been happening to your overall budget each year, you can do something about it. That's the exciting part. As one woman said, "I'm depressed and excited at the same time!"

Reminder

This worksheet is your guideline and is meant to be as flexible as possible. You are the one who decides how to utilize the worksheet and the information to your best advantage.

THE ONLINE/ELECTRONIC CONNECTION TO *THE BUDGET KIT*

Online Bill Payments

You can coordinate all of the information you gathered and listed for this **Yearly Budget Worksheet** with any online bill payment service you use (your bank's website or the website of the company itself). On the website, go to the "Payee List" and add the names (and all required information) of the companies or individuals you will be paying on a non-monthly, periodic basis throughout the year.

If you know the exact amount and date due for a particular expense, you can schedule them to be paid automatically. If you prefer to initiate the payment amount and date yourself, just add that final information when you know the funds are available to make the payment. Remember, allow at least five business days before the due date with all online bill payments.

Just like reviewing the **Yearly Budget Worksheet** on *page* 53, at the beginning of each month, you will visually be reminded of the bill and amount due whenever you pull up your "Pending Payments List." This is a great reminder for you to be prepared and make arrangements for upcoming expenses.

Online Budget Programs

Depending on the program you are using, you may be able to utilize this same concept and plan ahead for your periodic non-monthly expenses electronically. Try to set up the program to automatically set aside one-twelfth of the total periodic expenses into savings each month. Perhaps it will be easier to do the **Yearly Budget Worksheet** manually and then just plug in that monthly amount needed for savings. Or there may be a way on the program you are using that will do this automatically after you set up your periodic expenses.

SUGGESTION LIST—ADDITIONAL NON-MONTHLY EXPENSES

You can either complete this information here and then transfer it to the **Yearly Budget Worksheet** or use this as your guideline as you fill in the worksheet directly from these ideas.

Some of the expenses listed may be a monthly expense for you. If so, enter those expenses on the Monthly Budget Worksheet, *not here*. The focus of the Yearly Budget Worksheet is only on the *periodic, quarterly, semiannual, annual,* and *non-monthly* expenses.

	Description	Amount(s)	Months Due
Housing	Property Taxes		
	Homeowners Insurance/Renter's Insurance		
	Association/Condo Dues		
	Storage/Garage/PO Box		
	Yard/Garden Supplies		
	Yard Service/Maintenance		
	Pool Chemicals/Maintenance		
	Pest/Termite Control		
	Security System		
	Home Improvement Projects		
	Home Repairs/Maintenance		
	Carpet Cleaning/Window Cleaning		
	Dry Cleaning (drapes, bedding)		
	Home Furnishings/Decorating		
	Furniture/Appliances/Electronic Equipment		
	Maintenance Agreements		
	Other _____		
Utilities (Non-Monthly)	Fuel/Propane		
	Firewood		
	Waste Management		
	Water/Water Softener		
	Other _____		
Transportation	Vehicle #1 Insurance		
	Vehicle #2 Insurance		
	Boat/RV/Motorcycle Insurance & Expenses		
	Emission Inspection		
	License Renewal/Registration		
	Oil Change/Tune-up		
	Other Maintenance and Repairs		
	Other _____		
Health	Other Insurance		
	Medical Exams/Lab Tests		
	Visits (sick kids, allergy, etc.)		
	Physical Exam/School Physical		
	Prescriptions		
	Chiropractor		
	Dermatologist		
	Dental Exams/X-rays/Cleanings		
	Dental Work Needed		
	Orthodontia		
	Vision Exam/Glasses/Contacts		
	Alternative Health Practitioners		
	Vitamins/Supplements/Homeopathic		
	Other _____		

	Description	Amount(s)	Months Due
Insurance (Other)	Life Insurance	_____	_____
	Disability Insurance/Long-Term Care	_____	_____
	Other _____	_____	_____
Memberships	Church/Temple	_____	_____
	Country Club	_____	_____
	Credit Card Annual Fees	_____	_____
	Gym Annual Fees	_____	_____
	Organizations/Clubs	_____	_____
	Professional Dues/License	_____	_____
	Auto Club	_____	_____
	Sports	_____	_____
	Warehouse Clubs	_____	_____
	Other _____		_____
Computer/ Electronics	Hardware/Software	_____	_____
	Upgrades/Printer Supplies	_____	_____
	Service/Maintenance	_____	_____
	Classes/Training/Assistance	_____	_____
Education (Adult)	Tuition	_____	_____
	Book/Supply Expenses	_____	_____
	Trade Journals/Magazines/Newspapers	_____	_____
	Workshops/Seminars/Speakers	_____	_____
	Other _____	_____	_____
Clothing (Adults and Children)	Work Clothes/Uniforms/Shoes	_____	_____
	Seasonal Clothes/Shoes/Jackets	_____	_____
	Sports Clothes/Special Events	_____	_____
	Dry Cleaning/Alterations/Shoe Repair	_____	_____
Recreation (Adults)	Parties	_____	_____
	Concerts/Sports Events/Season Tickets	_____	_____
	Fees: Permits/Tournament/League	_____	_____
	Hobbies/Sports Equipment and Maintenance	_____	_____
	Lessons	_____	_____
	Other _____	_____	_____
Vacation/Trips	Transportation	_____	_____
	Lodging/Meals/Snacks	_____	_____
	Sights/Activities/Theatre/Galleries	_____	_____
	Shopping/Souvenirs/Film & Processing	_____	_____
Children	Tuition/College Expenses	_____	_____
	School Supplies	_____	_____
	Photos/Yearbooks/Class Ring/Letter Jacket	_____	_____
	Prom/Homecoming (flowers, hair, dinner, etc.)	_____	_____
	Field Trips/Contests/Expos/Fund-Raising/Fairs	_____	_____
	Camp Registration/Supplies	_____	_____
	Sports Equipment/Fees/Clinics	_____	_____
	Music Lessons/Equipment/Recitals/Costumes	_____	_____
	Other _____	_____	_____
Pets	Pet Food	_____	_____
	Grooming/Pet Hotel	_____	_____
	Vet Expense/Shots/Rx/Dental/Other	_____	_____
	Training/License	_____	_____
Misc.	Donations/Contributions	_____	_____
	Tax Preparation	_____	_____
	Taxes Due/Estimated Taxes	_____	_____
	Retirement Savings (IRA)	_____	_____

YEARLY BUDGET WORKSHEET

(Non-Monthly Anticipated Expenses)

FIXED AND ESTIMATED NON-MONTHLY EXPENSES

		JAN.	FEB.	MAR.	APR.	MAY	JUNE	JULY	AUG.	SEPT.	OCT.	NOV.	DEC.	TOTAL	MO. AVG.
Housing	Property Tax/ Homeowners Insurance														
	Home/Yard Maintenance			Door 250	Yard 150			Drapes 250						650	54
	Utilities	Sewer		65		20				50			85	220	18
Transportation	Auto Insurance	Van / Car		500 / 425						500 / 425				1,000 / 850	154
	Auto Expenses		Lube 25	Tires 250		Lube 25			Lube 25	Lic. 100	Lic. 80	Tune-up 150		655	55
Health	Insurance— Other	Life	80			80			80			80		320	27
	Medical Expenses	Rx 75		250		Dr. A 20			Rx 75			Lab 70		490	41
	Dental/Vision Expenses		Dental 750				Vis. 300		Dental 75					1,125	94
Additional Non-Monthly Expenses	Dues/Fees /Taxes		Prof. Lic. 95		Tax Prep 300		Ent. Bk 35	AAA 35	License 130			Gym 55		650	54
	Education/ Tuition	Student Loan	85	Seminar 150		85			85		Seminar 100	85		590	49
	Clothing- Child	Shoes/ Coat 320				350			400					1,070	89
	Recreation	Concert 60				Fish Lic. 35				Season Ticket 75				170	14
	Vacation/Trips		Ski 250				800					300		1,350	112
	Magazines		YM 16			Kip 20							BL 39	75	6
	Gifts—Birthday	25	15	50			15	100			100	75		380	32
	Gifts—Other	Anniv. 40			Grad. M. Day	60 50	F. Day 30		Shower 35		Wedding 40		Xmas 700	955	80
	Holiday Events				Easter 25			40			Halloween 60	TG 70	Xmas 400	595	50
	Children's Activities	65			Field Trip 100		Camp 150	Lessons 65		School 75	Photos 50			505	42
	Pets														
	Donations	15		WWF 25				G.P. 30			RC 50		CRS 100	220	18
	Personal	Spa 80			25			Spa 80			25			210	18
	Total	680	1,316	1,965	600	725	1,350	600	905	1,225	505	885	1,324	12,080	1,007

Reserve Savings: **Total Expenses $** 12,080 **÷ 12 = $** 1,006.67 **/Month** (Rounded Up)

YEARLY BUDGET WORKSHEET

(Non-Monthly Anticipated Expenses)

YEAR 20___

FIXED AND ESTIMATED NON-MONTHLY EXPENSES

		JAN.	FEB.	MAR.	APR.	MAY	JUNE	JULY	AUG.	SEPT.	OCT.	NOV.	DEC.	TOTAL	MO. AVG.
Housing	Property Tax/ Homeowners Insurance														
	Home/Yard Maintenance														
	Utilities														
Transportation	Auto Insurance														
	Auto Expenses														
Health	Insurance— Other														
	Medical Expenses														
	Dental/Vision Expenses														
Additional Non-Monthly Expenses	Dues/Fees														
	Education/ Tuition														
	Clothing-														
	Recreation														
	Vacation/Trips														
	Gifts—Birthday														
	Gifts—Other														
	Holiday Events														
	Children's Activities														
	Pets														
	Total														

Reserve Savings: Total Expenses $ _____ ÷ 12 = $ _____ /Month

Gift Giving Worksheet

Gift giving is often one of the most underestimated and overlooked budget categories in many households. People often are amazed, once they start recording all their expenses, just how much money actually is spent on gifts. It is not uncommon to forget occasional events or extended family members or *teachers, bosses, hairdressers,* and *pets* on this gift list when trying to estimate the overall gift budget.

This **Gift Giving Worksheet** works as a reminder of often forgotten expenses as you anticipate the total yearly cost for all upcoming events involving gifts. Remembering Christmas and birthdays generally is easy. Events such as Father's Day or your parents' anniversary, however, often are overlooked until the month they occur. Even if you don't buy gifts but send flowers or go out to dinner instead, include these costs in your plan. By outlining all the members of your family and your friends and all the events celebrated in your household on this worksheet, and how much you want to budget for each, you will have a handy total picture of what gift expenses to expect. You then can transfer these amounts to the "Gifts" section of the **Yearly Budget Worksheet** under the appropriate months.

As you think of gift ideas, you could add them in small print to this form as well.

GIFT GIVING WORKSHEET

	Name	Amount: Christmas/ Hanukkah	Amount: Birthday	Actual Month Due	Other Events Happening*	Amount: Other Events	Actual Month Due
Spouse		$	$			$	
Parents/Self							
Children/Grandchildren							
Sisters/Brothers							

*Other: Anniversaries, weddings, showers, babies, Mother's Day, Father's Day, graduations, Bar Mitzvahs, religious events

GIFT GIVING WORKSHEET

	Name	Amount: Christmas/ Hanukkah	Amount: Birthday	Actual Month Due	Other Events Happening*	Amount: Other Events	Actual Month Due
Grandparents		$	$			$	
Aunts/Uncles							
Nieces/Nephews							
Friends/Work/Other							
Children's Friends							
	Total of both pages	$	$			$	

*Other: Anniversaries, weddings, showers, babies, Mother's Day, Father's Day, graduations, Bar Mitzvahs, religious events

CHRISTMAS/HOLIDAY EXPENSE WORKSHEET

Item	Estimate	Already Have	Actual Cost
Tree/Wreath			
Lights–House/Tree			
Baked Goods/Ginger House			
Parties/Food/Liquor/Beverage Host Gifts			
Poinsettias/Candles Decorations/Crafts			
Gift Wrap Greeting Cards			
Postage Shipping/Boxes			
Digital Photo Processing/Family Portraits			
Clothes/Shoes/Jewelry			
Meals Out			
Movies/Ballet/Plays/Galleries Travel/Tour			
Workplace Events			
Donations			
Batteries/Misc. (for gifts) Other			
Total Amount			

SOURCE OF MONEY FOR GIFTS AND HOLIDAY EXPENSES

Amount Needed

Total Amount for Gifts:
   (See Gift Giving Worksheet) $_____

Total Amount–Holiday Expenses:
   (See worksheet above) $_____

TOTAL AMOUNT NEEDED
   for Gifts and Holiday Expenses: $_____

List how much is available from the following sources to cover these holiday expenses:

Total Amount Available		
Source	**Amount**	**Notes**
Current Income		
Overtime/Part-time Job		
Savings Account(s)		
Gift Money/Bonus		
Total Amount Available to Cover Expenses		
Total Amount Needed for Gifts & Holiday Expenses		
Amount Short/Extra*		

*Total Amount Needed – Total Amount Available to Cover Expenses = Amount Short or Extra

Outline a plan for covering amount that is short for holiday expenses:

Source	**Amount**	**Notes**
Overtime/Part Time Job		
Charge on Credit Cards		
Borrow		
Other		
Total Amount Need to Borrow		

Monthly Budget Worksheet

Why a Monthly Budget Worksheet?

The Monthly Budget Worksheet is designed to provide a guideline for coordinating your monthly bills and expenses with your *take-home* pay. Your monthly bills are often easier to remember because most bills come in the mail or through email. Forgotten, however, are the expenses each month such as meals eaten out, haircuts, gifts, books, DVDs, seminars, and the like that often throw off the monthly budget.

This worksheet is especially helpful during those lean times when your income is reduced and the amount of bills to pay exceeds the money coming in. This guideline will give you a better overall picture of your monthly obligations and lifestyle expenses. The categories are kept general to allow for flexibility and necessary additions based on your own personal financial needs.

Often something as simple as this worksheet can be the difference between financial chaos and financial control. For the Mathews the true test came when the commission check was exceptionally low one month. After months of working diligently on their budget, this young, ambitious couple had the skills and tools to tighten up and be creative about their spending. They knew what to do. Banana bread was made at home to replace the sales meeting bagels, all meals out were eliminated, brown bag meals and soggy sandwiches replaced the business meals out while on the road, and all other discretionary spending was cut back. By the end of the month the Mathews were ecstatic as they made it through the month financially intact—all the bills were paid, good meals were eaten at home, no credit card charges, no little loans, and, best of all, they felt totally motivated by their ability to take control of the situation.

How to Get Started

To use the Monthly Budget Worksheet, look at the filled in sample on *page 67* and follow these instructions. Start with the top row next to "Income Source" and indicate in each column where your money is coming from for that month, whether it is from your job, your spouse's job, your checkbook balance rolled over from the previous month, investment or rental income, savings, a refund, and so on.

Next, on the second row next to "Net Income Total Amount" ①, write down the *net amount* of each paycheck or source of other money that will be used to pay for those monthly expenses. How many columns you fill in depends on how often you are paid each month. Of course, there are many job situations where the amount may vary or is not always known, such as with commission sales. If this is the case, make a very *conservative* estimate until the actual amount is known. If your income is very erratic, you also can work with the **Variable Income Worksheet** following this section.

You will notice the emphasis on net income and not on gross income throughout the workbook. This way, you are dealing only with the cash you actually have for paying your bills. Your payroll deductions and taxes are not being ignored. You can record that information on the **Monthly Expense Record** as well as on the **End-of-the-Year Tax Information** form on *page* 147.

On the third row under the "Income Source" amount there is room to add the **date** ② each paycheck is received. This will help with your planning when working around due dates and paying your bills.

Finally, total all of the income and other sources of money across the top row and enter that total amount in the box at the bottom left corner of the page right next to "Total Income." ⑤

What Makes this Worksheet Unique

Now let's look at all those bills. List every bill and expense you can think of that will be coming up for that particular month in the second column called "Amount." ③ Included will be the obvious bills as well as the incidental, like planning to buy a new suit, attending a workshop, or having someone service your computer that month. This is not necessarily an *average* monthly budget that is being developed. And although it may well turn out to be an average monthly budget, the real purpose here is to take time to outline the specific month coming up and look at all of its unique variable expenses beyond the average amounts. For example, if your relatives are coming to visit for a week next month, your grocery, meals out, utility, gasoline, and entertainment amounts may all be higher than usual that month.

This proactive planning approach is what makes this budgeting process more unique than the standard method of taking the yearly total of expenses and dividing it by 12 months for a monthly average.

The other unique feature is learning how to coordinate the timing of the income with the due dates and needs of the expenses using this worksheet. I have had numerous clients finally "get it" when they saw how to work the payments and general expenses according to the timing of the income. *They no longer had to try to pay all their bills with the first paycheck out of fear of running out of money and then figure out how to live the next few weeks with limited money until they were paid again.*

Other clients used this worksheet to determine ahead of time how much cash to pull out for each week for various cash expenses and eliminated all the incidental nonplanned runs to the ATM machine.

This worksheet will definitely help you become proactive and more relaxed in your approach to managing money instead of staying in a reactive mode.

So now let's review how to fill in the expenses in the column under the "Amount" heading. The Sample page on *page* 67 will help you get a better idea.

Pay Yourself First

Notice that "Allowance/Mad Money" ④ and "Savings" are under "Fixed Amounts." The phrase "pay yourself first" has been said many times. It is a valid statement and a very important rule because if you penny-pinch to the point where there is no money left for "Allowance/Mad Money," you will end up bickering, frustrated, and disappointed with the whole budget idea. The "Allowance/Mad Money" should be yours to do with as you please. Decide how much "Allowance/Mad Money" each member needs in order to allow for little splurges and yet not ignore the necessary expenses.

Just as important under "Fixed Amounts" is "Savings." Again, this is paying yourself first. Consider "Savings" as an *expense*, setting aside a specific amount or percentage of your check at the same time you are completing the other categories of the worksheet. In this manner, you will be thinking of "Savings" as an expense so that it is planned for regularly and not dependent on leftover funds.

Remember the different savings accounts—**reserve** (for upcoming known bills and expenses listed on the **Yearly Budget Worksheet**), **emergency** (equivalent to at least three months of take-home pay for unknown disasters), and **goals** (wish list)—and try to save regularly for them. See the **Savings Activity Record** on *page* 170 for tracking your savings.

Once you have saved enough money for the reserve and emergency accounts, you will realize that it is actually possible to save money. Saving for your goals soon becomes more exciting and challenging as you realize that reaching your goals now is possible.

Now for Some Practice at Budgeting

In many cases, such as utilities or other areas under "Fixed Variable" and "Occasional," the exact amount of the bill is unknown. For those categories, this is where your budgeting practice comes in as you estimate the bills until the exact amount is known. Remember to keep in mind those other expenses that are not seen as bills but show up on a daily basis: groceries, gas, entertainment, clothing, and so on. Those must be planned for as well. Here you will take an estimated guess (budget) as to what you will need and the amount you can spend. If you use the **Monthly Expense Record** starting on *page* 120 for tracking your expenses each month, you will have a better sense of some averages to use for these categories when estimating. Once you become familiar with estimating your expenditures, you will successfully begin to live within your budget. If your budget is realistic, you soon will choose to eliminate certain unnecessary items to remain within the projected budget.

More Month than Money—Now What?

Before you total the "Amount" column, think again if there is anything else that may be coming up as an expense for the particular month you are outlining. Look at the categories on the **Monthly Expense Record** and the **Suggestion List— Additional Non-Monthly Expenses** in the **Yearly Budget Worksheet** section and see if any ideas are triggered for possible expenses. And finally, look at the **Yearly Budget Worksheet**. If you have not put the 1/12th into reserve savings, did you include those unique expenses when planning for this particular month?

Now it's time to tally up and face the total. Put that total figure for this column "Amount" at the bottom next to "Total Expenses." ⑤ As you filled in this column you probably were already telling yourself this is more than you have coming in. If that is the case, at least now you can see it in black and white and know why some of the months have been running short and why those expenses probably ended up on the credit cards.

Remember, *this worksheet is done before the month ever begins*. It is a projection of your anticipated budget. That means you now have the time and opportunity to take charge and do something about this information. You always have the following choices: postpone, cut back, eliminate, or find creative alternatives.

Contact the creditors and see what special arrangements you can make. Many will accommodate you and allow postponed or partial payments if you notify them. What can you eliminate? Lattes, books, CDs, meals out, full-price movies, clothes, and gadgets are starters. Go through and reevaluate each expense.

What else can you do? How can you bring more money in? Can you get more overtime hours or a part-time job? Do you have enough "stuff" to have a yard sale? What if you took your unused books, CDs, and clothes to the resale shops for some extra cash?

In the meantime, possibly you have been building a small emergency fund and can cover part or all of the expenses this time by withdrawing the necessary amount. This should be an absolute last resort, however, with cutbacks planned for the next few months so that you can replenish your emergency fund once again.

Timing Income with Payments and Expenses

Now that you have reworked your numbers so your expenses match your income, go back to the top of the "Amount" column in the "Fixed Amounts" section. Distribute and balance the more expensive bills over the different pay periods in each column, as you fill in the amounts, *based on due dates and income dates*. If some pay periods, like the beginning of the month, are pretty top heavy with bills, try contacting the creditor and see about arranging to change the date according to your next paycheck for future payments.

Another method is to allocate small portions from some or all of the paychecks to cover a large bill, such as the mortgage. What some readers have done in those cases is to itemize a portion under different pay periods and then write a check for that amount and keep it in the envelope until the final check and full amount is ready. They then sent the envelope with the multiple checks totaling the complete payment.

Categories like groceries, gasoline, and meals out are generally divided somewhat under each pay period. You decide how best to balance all the expenses under each of the "Income" columns. *Working with pencil* will again be preferred, as it may take some fine-tuning to balance each of the "Income" columns with the expenses.

Customizing the Income Columns for your Household

It is always fascinating to learn the different ways clients and readers have found to utilize the full functionality of this worksheet. Listed below are a few ways to adapt this worksheet, primarily the "Income" columns, so it works best for your household and financial situation.

Checking Account Balance

Since most households roll over to the next month with some balance in the checking account before the next paycheck arrives, it would make sense to replace the first column labeled "Chris" and designate it "Account Balance." This amount is the money available to handle the most immediate expense needs the first week of the month.

Credit Card Use

There are two aspects to this approach. The first addresses the deliberate and conscious use of the credit card by putting the majority of major expenses on the credit card. This leverages the card mileage and other benefits, offers the convenience of paying one check for all the expenses (and paying off the credit card in full), and having most of the spending records on one statement. Therefore, the second column labeled "Kim" can be designated instead as "Credit Card" and all the expenses under the "Amount" column that are paid with the credit card are then also listed under this "Credit Card" column.

The second aspect of this approach is using the credit card as "supplemental income." It is important to recognize this practice for what it is and understand that you are truly using the credit card for your "supplemental income," and technically borrowing money to get through the month. The goal obviously, is to get to the point where you are balancing your income and your spending and not continuing with this risky practice too long. In the meantime, the way to use this **Monthly Budget Worksheet** proactively to best understand and to stay conscious of what you are doing through this whole exercise, is to use one column designated for "credit card" use only. This helps you to identify which critical expenses will have to fall on the credit card this particular month in order to make it through the month in tact. This solution is used only after all other adjustments and arrangements are handled in the initial planning discussed earlier, and there is still a shortage for the month. Ideally, when you plan out the following month, you will be sure to find a way to add more to your credit card payment expense.

Reimbursements

Dealing with business reimbursements for your job in some cases can get a little crazy and confusing depending on timing and actual amounts reimbursed. Since all of these situations are so variable, find a way to make this work best for your situation. Create a column designated for the anticipated amount of the reimbursement for the month you are planning. List what your total expense needs are going to be for the current upcoming month you are planning under the "Amount" column. You then have a way to show how some or all of those expenses can be covered with the previous reimbursement check coming in for the current month and keep that business expense category more separated in the household budget.

Bonus—Overtime—Gift Money

During those months you happen to have extra money from a variety of sources, designate a column with this title and then determine how you will prioritize and best use this money for the expenses during the month you are planning. Perhaps a big chunk will be added in the savings section. In this case, you would be sure to list the amount of savings as one of your "Expenses" under the "Amount" column and then show that amount again on the column you designate as "Bonus." Or, you may add an additional amount to the credit card payment and show part of the payment from your usual paycheck and then a second payment from this bonus money.

For more ideas on how to best distribute your bonus money with a plan rather than react to all the spending temptations, be sure to see the **Windfall Planner** on *page* 90 before making any decisions.

Cash

If you're having a hard time determining how much cash you need each month and how you will use cash only, designate one of the remaining columns as "Cash." When you finish outlining all of your expenses and coordinating the bills based on due dates, review the list and notice which areas you tend to use mostly cash (lunches out, church donations, bottled water). Next, list each of these amounts under the "Cash" column. Be sure to put a dollar amount for this cash at the top on the "Net Income Total Amount" line. In this case, if the cash is coming from a paycheck, you will also need to be sure you subtracted that same amount from the net paycheck amount listed on the income column.

Getting Control of your Finances

You have just completed an important step in getting and keeping control of your finances. Of course, doing a Monthly Budget Worksheet does not change or increase the amount of actual money earned. Being aware, however, of where and how the money is spent will give you the feeling that you are beginning to control your money and will help you stretch the use of those dollars more than ever before.

Happy budgeting!

"I was shocked into action when I worked out my budget on the Monthly Budget Worksheet and realized I was $1,000 short. Now after four years all our bills are paid in full and we are completely out of debt. Without putting information down on paper every month, I don't think I could have done it."

THE ONLINE/ELECTRONIC CONNECTION TO *THE BUDGET KIT*

Online Bill Payments

This **Monthly Budget Worksheet** is actually an *ideal tool* to use if you are ready to simplify the bill payment process but prefer to continue using the hands-on system for outlining your monthly bills and expenses. Visually, you have everything down on one sheet and can easily see the amounts and dates for each of the bills.

To streamline the process of actually paying all those bills, you have a number of convenient cashless choices. You may already be using automatic bank withdrawals for utilities and loan payments on your home, cars, and other loans. Many people also choose to use their credit card for automatically paying fixed and regular monthly bills. They then pay the bill in full, enjoying the convenience and other benefits they receive by using a particular credit card.

Often, there are still payments due to small businesses and individuals who will only take checks. This is where online bill payment services through your bank or other service providers truly distinguish themselves. A majority of the services will pay any bill for you. Once you have signed up for the online service, all you have to do is enter the information for your new payee, indicate which account to use, how much to pay and when, and you are finished.

continued on next page

THE ONLINE/ELECTRONIC CONNECTION TO *THE BUDGET KIT* continued

A final note if you aren't quite ready to start paying your bills online. It is very likely that your bank offers online banking. That means you can check your current balance and see what checks have cleared at anytime as you work out your plan with the **Monthly Budget Worksheet**. This may be the perfect way for you to slowly transition to online financial services.

Online Budget Programs

Most programs will have some method of setting up a budget for the month tied into the online bill payment service. Use this **Monthly Budget Worksheet** as a way to plan out your online program more comprehensively and as a reminder of all the categories of expenses to include for the month when setting up your budget online. Once all your information is in place and your various online financial accounts are set up, the system should automatically retrieve and set up all your spending and deposit records in one place every time you log on. Whether you use credit cards, debit cards, ATMs or checks, you should be able to assign each transaction to the correct category with just a click of your mouse or some transactions may assign automatically. Ideally, when everything is set up, this system will handle all your fixed, variable, and incidental bills seamlessly.

Since most programs are going to help you see what you have spent and where you stand financially at any given time, it will still be up to you to outline a plan ahead of time that incorporates all of your upcoming monthly needs. You can use this **Monthly Budget Worksheet** as a guideline for determining the timing of your bills, based on your income and other money coming in to be sure your income carries you through the month. This worksheet will also help you outline ahead of time how much money you want to pull out ahead for cash expenses.

Monthly Budget Worksheet on Excel

When readers and clients started using this worksheet they noticed a dramatic difference in their planning and spending. Because of the variability in each household, there is usually more adjusting with the rows for the listed expenses or with the columns for the different income sources and planning systems. This is one of the core worksheets available on Excel and looks exactly the same way on the screen with a separate tab on the bottom for every month. It is available at *http://moneytracker.com/books-TheBudgetKitExcel.htm*. The true value of using Excel, beyond the quick calculations, is the ability to add and adjust the rows and columns more conveniently.

MONTHLY BUDGET WORKSHEET

SAMPLE

INCOME SOURCE:				Chris	Kim	Chris	Kim	Savings Reserve
① Net Income Total Amount				896	1,407	880	1,407	1,380

	Expenses	③ Amount	Date Due	Date Paid	Date ② Rcv.: 9/4	9/7	9/18	9/21	9/15
Fixed Amounts	Mortgage/Rent	784	10	4	784				
	Car Payments	291	15	10		291			
	Other Loans student	167	15	10		167			
	Internet Access								
	Day Care								
	Insurance Auto	500*	10	6					500
	Auto	425*	10	6					425
	Clubs/Dues								
	Savings Emergency	215						115	
	Savings Goals	75				100		75	
④	Savings Reserve	1,007				400	300	307	
	Allowance/Mad Money	50			20		30		
Fixed Variable	Electricity	75	20	18			75		
	Oil/Gas	45	25	20			45		
	Water/Garbage	125*	11	6					125
	Telephone/Cell Phone	65	27	20			65		
	Cable TV/Satellite	35	25	20			35		
	Groceries	450			50	150	50	200	
	Meals Out	125				30	50	45	
	Auto Expense/Gas	85				30	30	25	
	Auto License	100*							100
	Activities	30							
	Child Allowance	40			10	10	10	40	
	Church/Charity	325				70		255	
Occasional	Household Photos	20					20		
	Personal Spa	80*							80
	Clothes /Dry Cleaning	75/35			25	35		50	
	Medical Prescrip.	35				35			
	Child Expense School Exp.	75*							75
	Recreation Season Ticket	75*							75
	Counseling	130				65		65	
	Books, CDs, Movies/Videos	90			10		25		
Installment	Credit Cards	55				25		30	
	Visa	100	25	20			100		
	MC	200	27	20				200	
Total ⑤	Total Income	4,590							
	Total Expense Excludes*	4,549			899	1,408	835	1,407	1,380
	Total Excess	41					45		
	Total Short				–3	–1			

Expenses showing an * are paid from Reserve Savings (Yearly Budget Worksheet) and not included in this Total Expense figure.

MONTHLY BUDGET WORKSHEET

INCOME SOURCE:			Date		Date					
Net Income Total Amount:										
Expenses	**Amount**	**Due**	**Paid**	**Rcv.:**						

	Expenses	Amount	Due	Paid	Rcv.:				
Fixed Amounts	Mortgage/Rent								
	Car Payments								
	Other Loans								
	Internet Access								
	Day Care								
	Insurance								
	Clubs/Dues								
	Savings								
	Allowance/Mad Money								
Fixed Variable	Electricity								
	Oil/Gas								
	Water/Garbage								
	Telephone/Cell Phone								
	Cable TV/Satellite								
	Groceries								
	Meals Out								
	Auto Expense/Gas								
	Church/Charity								
Occasional	Household								
	Personal								
	Clothes								
	Medical								
	Child Expense								
	Recreation								
Installment	Credit Cards								
Total	**Total Income**								
	Total Expense								
	Total Excess								
	Total Short								

MONTHLY BUDGET WORKSHEET

INCOME SOURCE:									
Net Income Total Amount:									

	Expenses	Amount	Date Due	Date Paid	Date Rcv.:				
Fixed Amounts	Mortgage/Rent								
	Car Payments								
	Other Loans								
	Internet Access								
	Day Care								
	Insurance								
	Clubs/Dues								
	Savings								
	Allowance/Mad Money								
Fixed Variable	Electricity								
	Oil/Gas								
	Water/Garbage								
	Telephone/Cell Phone								
	Cable TV/Satellite								
	Groceries								
	Meals Out								
	Auto Expense/Gas								
	Church/Charity								
Occasional	Household								
	Personal								
	Clothes								
	Medical								
	Child Expense								
	Recreation								
Installment	Credit Cards								
Total	Total Income								
	Total Expense								
	Total Excess								
	Total Short								

MONTHLY BUDGET WORKSHEET

	INCOME SOURCE:								
	Net Income Total Amount:								
	Expenses	**Amount**	Date **Due**	**Paid**	Date **Rcv.:**				
Fixed Amounts	Mortgage/Rent								
	Car Payments								
	Other Loans								
	Internet Access								
	Day Care								
	Insurance								
	Clubs/Dues								
	Savings								
	Allowance/Mad Money								
Fixed Variable	Electricity								
	Oil/Gas								
	Water/Garbage								
	Telephone/Cell Phone								
	Cable TV/Satellite								
	Groceries								
	Meals Out								
	Auto Expense/Gas								
	Church/Charity								
Occasional	Household								
	Personal								
	Clothes								
	Medical								
	Child Expense								
	Recreation								
Installment	Credit Cards								
Total	**Total Income**								
	Total Expense								
	Total Excess								
	Total Short								

MONTHLY BUDGET WORKSHEET

APRIL

INCOME SOURCE:									
Net Income Total Amount:									

	Expenses	Amount	Date Due	Date Paid	Date Rcv.:				
Fixed Amounts	Mortgage/Rent								
	Car Payments								
	Other Loans								
	Internet Access								
	Day Care								
	Insurance								
	Clubs/Dues								
	Savings								
	Allowance/Mad Money								
Fixed Variable	Electricity								
	Oil/Gas								
	Water/Garbage								
	Telephone/Cell Phone								
	Cable TV/Satellite								
	Groceries								
	Meals Out								
	Auto Expense/Gas								
	Church/Charity								
Occasional	Household								
	Personal								
	Clothes								
	Medical								
	Child Expense								
	Recreation								
Installment	Credit Cards								
Total	Total Income								
	Total Expense								
	Total Excess								
	Total Short								

MONTHLY BUDGET WORKSHEET

INCOME SOURCE:								
Net Income Total Amount:								

	Expenses	Amount	Date Due	Date Paid	Date Rcv.:			
Fixed Amounts	Mortgage/Rent							
	Car Payments							
	Other Loans							
	Internet Access							
	Day Care							
	Insurance							
	Clubs/Dues							
	Savings							
	Allowance/Mad Money							
Fixed Variable	Electricity							
	Oil/Gas							
	Water/Garbage							
	Telephone/Cell Phone							
	Cable TV/Satellite							
	Groceries							
	Meals Out							
	Auto Expense/Gas							
	Church/Charity							
Occasional	Household							
	Personal							
	Clothes							
	Medical							
	Child Expense							
	Recreation							
Installment	Credit Cards							
Total	Total Income							
	Total Expense							
	Total Excess							
	Total Short							

INCOME SOURCE:								
Net Income Total Amount:								

	Expenses	Amount	Date Due	Date Paid	Date Rcv.:				
Fixed Amounts	Mortgage/Rent								
	Car Payments								
	Other Loans								
	Internet Access								
	Day Care								
	Insurance								
	Clubs/Dues								
	Savings								
	Allowance/Mad Money								
Fixed Variable	Electricity								
	Oil/Gas								
	Water/Garbage								
	Telephone/Cell Phone								
	Cable TV/Satellite								
	Groceries								
	Meals Out								
	Auto Expense/Gas								
	Church/Charity								
Occasional	Household								
	Personal								
	Clothes								
	Medical								
	Child Expense								
	Recreation								
Installment	Credit Cards								
Total	**Total Income**								
	Total Expense								
	Total Excess								
	Total Short								

MONTHLY BUDGET WORKSHEET

INCOME SOURCE:								
Net Income Total Amount:								

	Expenses	Amount	Date Due	Date Paid	Date Rcv.:				
Fixed Amounts	Mortgage/Rent								
	Car Payments								
	Other Loans								
	Internet Access								
	Day Care								
	Insurance								
	Clubs/Dues								
	Savings								
	Allowance/Mad Money								
Fixed Variable	Electricity								
	Oil/Gas								
	Water/Garbage								
	Telephone/Cell Phone								
	Cable TV/Satellite								
	Groceries								
	Meals Out								
	Auto Expense/Gas								
	Church/Charity								
Occasional	Household								
	Personal								
	Clothes								
	Medical								
	Child Expense								
	Recreation								
Installment	Credit Cards								
Total	**Total Income**								
	Total Expense								
	Total Excess								
	Total Short								

MONTHLY BUDGET WORKSHEET

INCOME SOURCE:									
Net Income Total Amount:									

	Expenses	Amount	Date Due	Date Paid	Date Rcv.:				
Fixed Amounts	Mortgage/Rent								
	Car Payments								
	Other Loans								
	Internet Access								
	Day Care								
	Insurance								
	Clubs/Dues								
	Savings								
	Allowance/Mad Money								
Fixed Variable	Electricity								
	Oil/Gas								
	Water/Garbage								
	Telephone/Cell Phone								
	Cable TV/Satellite								
	Groceries								
	Meals Out								
	Auto Expense/Gas								
	Church/Charity								
Occasional	Household								
	Personal								
	Clothes								
	Medical								
	Child Expense								
	Recreation								
Installment	Credit Cards								
Total	Total Income								
	Total Expense								
	Total Excess								
	Total Short								

MONTHLY BUDGET WORKSHEET

SEPTEMBER

INCOME SOURCE:								
Net Income Total Amount:								

	Expenses	Amount	Date Due	Date Paid	Date Rcv.:			
Fixed Amounts	Mortgage/Rent							
	Car Payments							
	Other Loans							
	Internet Access							
	Day Care							
	Insurance							
	Clubs/Dues							
	Savings							
	Allowance/Mad Money							
Fixed Variable	Electricity							
	Oil/Gas							
	Water/Garbage							
	Telephone/Cell Phone							
	Cable TV/Satellite							
	Groceries							
	Meals Out							
	Auto Expense/Gas							
	Church/Charity							
Occasional	Household							
	Personal							
	Clothes							
	Medical							
	Child Expense							
	Recreation							
Installment	Credit Cards							
Total	**Total Income**							
	Total Expense							
	Total Excess							
	Total Short							

MONTHLY BUDGET WORKSHEET

	Expenses	Amount	Date Due	Date Paid	Date Rcv.:				
Fixed Amounts	Mortgage/Rent	230. 1	1/35	26/011	10/1				
	Car Payments	7	10+ +	1/11					
	Other Loans								
	Internet Access								
	Day Care								
	Insurance								
	Clubs/Dues								
	Savings								
	Allowance/Mad Money								
Fixed Variable	Electricity								
	Oil/Gas								
	Water/Garbage								
	Telephone/Cell Phone								
	Cable TV/Satellite								
	Groceries								
	Meals Out								
	Auto Expense/Gas								
	Church/Charity								
Occasional	Household								
	Personal								
	Clothes								
	Medical								
	Child Expense								
	Recreation								
Installment	Credit Cards								
Total	**Total Income**								
	Total Expense								
	Total Excess								
	Total Short								

INCOME SOURCE:
Net Income Total Amount:

MONTHLY BUDGET WORKSHEET

INCOME SOURCE:									
Net Income Total Amount:									

	Expenses	Amount	Date Due	Date Paid	Date Rcv.:				
Fixed Amounts	Mortgage/Rent								
	Car Payments								
	Other Loans								
	Internet Access								
	Day Care								
	Insurance								
	Clubs/Dues								
	Savings								
	Allowance/Mad Money								
Fixed Variable	Electricity								
	Oil/Gas								
	Water/Garbage								
	Telephone/Cell Phone								
	Cable TV/Satellite								
	Groceries								
	Meals Out								
	Auto Expense/Gas								
	Church/Charity								
Occasional	Household								
	Personal								
	Clothes								
	Medical								
	Child Expense								
	Recreation								
Installment	Credit Cards								
Total	**Total Income**								
	Total Expense								
	Total Excess								
	Total Short								

	INCOME SOURCE:							
	Net Income Total Amount:							

	Expenses	Amount	Date Due	Date Paid	Date Rcv.:			
Fixed Amounts	Mortgage/Rent							
	Car Payments							
	Other Loans							
	Internet Access							
	Day Care							
	Insurance							
	Clubs/Dues							
	Savings							
	Allowance/Mad Money							
Fixed Variable	Electricity							
	Oil/Gas							
	Water/Garbage							
	Telephone/Cell Phone							
	Cable TV/Satellite							
	Groceries							
	Meals Out							
	Auto Expense/Gas							
	Church/Charity							
Occasional	Household							
	Personal							
	Clothes							
	Medical							
	Child Expense							
	Recreation							
Installment	Credit Cards							
Total	Total Income							
	Total Expense							
	Total Excess							
	Total Short							

Variable Income Worksheet

Planning your monthly finances can be especially challenging when your income is not predictable or regular each month. Often I hear people say they cannot create a budget because their income is based on commissions, self-employment, or other irregular income and therefore they feel they have no way to plan ahead. Actually, having a spending plan that gives you a clear outline of your basic monthly fixed expenses and a plan for covering them is even *more* important when your income is not regular.

I have met with many clients who have been in variable income situations, which is the reason I added this new worksheet. For many of those clients, utilizing all three of the main worksheets together—the **Yearly Budget Worksheet, Monthly Budget Worksheet**, and **Monthly Expense Record** (found in this section of the workbook)—worked most effectively. They were able to get a handle on the best approach for dealing with those three-month stretches of no income and then successfully plan the best way to distribute the bonus check or commission or other business income when it did come in.

This worksheet is designed to give you a guideline for planning a system that helps you know and cover your basic fixed monthly expenses every month, whether you receive income or not. Without a clear long-range plan, it is very tempting to react to a large sum of money as a mini windfall. This worksheet will help you keep a big-picture perspective. You will learn to plan proactively and stay prepared for upcoming financial obligations by saving the appropriate amount of money.

The key is starting with a conservative approach and stashing as much of the income as possible into savings to act as your future monthly income. This is especially true if you do not really know when the next amount of money will be coming in or how much. You may only know that it is very likely that the case will be settled, or the sale will close, or the partnership may have enough to pay salaries again, or the company will be giving some bonus distribution at some point. And yes, there is always the possibility that something can happen and the money may *not* come through.

That's why you want contingency plans: money in the bank; ability to cut back dramatically with the spending; good credit rating to help with access to loans; back-up help from family or friends; other job possibilities; good relationships with all your creditors to work out short-term arrangements; attention to your investments to be sure they are performing well; and a reality check on the real cost of your cars and other personal property that you may want to sell or replace with less expensive versions.

As you work out the history or the current record of your irregular income, you may see that there actually is a pattern. With this pattern you can begin to coordinate some of your big-ticket payments, such as annual or semiannual insurances, tuition, or taxes, with the timing of the income. Clients have often been amazed to realize how much power they had over their finances once they were armed with information. Many times you can make arrangements for totally different payment dates and even payments if you have a clear outlined plan and you discuss it with a receptive customer service representative or supervisor for that company.

There may be many months when no money is coming in and you are living solely on the savings you have set aside specifically for those months. Continue to stay conscious of your spending and money patterns during this time. Even though living that way can be unsettling, remember to pat yourself on the back for having the foresight and prudence to put sufficient funds aside.

How to Use this Worksheet

The purpose of the **Variable Income Worksheet** is twofold. First, it serves as a planner for projecting upcoming income to the best of your ability. Second, once the actual income comes in and you record this information, you will have a record to refer to next year when projecting the new year. I usually suggest you use pencil or have a way to easily change your numbers because this whole book is a *workbook* and your work is always in progress.

Windfall Planner

Before starting on this Variable Income Worksheet it may help to review the **Windfall Planner** worksheet on *page* 90. The Windfall Planner is helpful for those one-time lump sums of money, such as an insurance settlement, inheritance, or company bonus. Using that planner helps you to see the many options to consider and to then prioritize the distribution of those funds.

Multiple Sales Monthly Planner

If you are in sales, before you begin this Variable Income Worksheet I want you to know about the **Multiple Sales Monthly Planner** on *pages* 92–94. As you know, variable commission income could be from multiple closings on products and projects as well as from one big commission check. To help itemize all those different possible closing amounts, I have added an accessory planner. With this planner, you will have a way to record those sales that are projected, listed, pending, or sold for each month. Once you have completed the total amount of actual closings, you can transfer that monthly total to the Variable Income Worksheet under "Income Source."

Income Source

A variety of income sources are listed on *page 86*. If your source does not fit any of these categories, cross them out and insert your own. When you know the amount or approximate amount of the bonus, commission, or other income source and the month, enter that amount in the column under the appropriate month.

If you know the month but have no clue what the figure will be, like dividends or royalties, only that some amount will be coming in, place an "X" in the box under the month to remind you when some money will be arriving. This also acts as a reminder in the event some expected money has not arrived and you can then follow up on the delay.

Once that large check does arrive, the critical step is to evaluate how best to distribute those funds. What do you pay off first? How much do you save? How much do you need to live on for this month and possibly many more months? The following sections will help you determine the best ways to use the money, including how much money you will need, how much to put aside in savings, and how much debt you can pay off.

Estimated Taxes/Savings

After you finish relishing the nice bonus package or commission check that just came in, remember that the very next step is addressing the taxes. If taxes have not been withdrawn from this particular source of income, then this is the place to start and make sure you calculate how much to put aside for taxes. Enter this amount on *page 87* on the top row.

There are enough resources to advise you where the best place is for "parking" your money while saving it. You may already work with a tax accountant or financial planner who can advise you on where and how much to save. As a general guideline, I recommend putting aside approximately 25 to 30 percent as a minimum starting place for your basic commissions and other job income. The most important point is to do it. Move that money over to savings, a money market account, CD, or whatever seems most appropriate right away so you are dealing with realistic numbers as you plan your budget. Some people find it easier to dedicate a separate savings account for taxes only so they are not tempted to use that money for other household expenses or emergencies.

The goal throughout this workbook is to help you to manage your finances proactively instead of reactively. Ignoring the tax issue or saying you will take more money out of the next check for taxes because this time you really need all the money, starts to set you up for that reactive crisis management cycle once again. This time you can change that cycle. Be patient and know you *can* turn things around. Outline this plan and follow it as closely as you can.

Note About Stock Options

In this world of stock options and other huge money packages, it is more important than ever to pay attention to the tax consequences. It is not unusual to see more than 50 percent in the end going to taxes depending on your income bracket and other factors. I have witnessed a lot of financial havoc for clients who had not withdrawn enough for taxes. Large sums of money can easily draw you in emotionally and skew your good judgement. Be sure to talk with a tax accountant for an accurate projection before buying that new car with cash.

Fixed and Variable Expenses

The next step on *page* 87 is addressing the "Basic Monthly Household and Personal Expenses" part of the worksheet. I recommend completing the **Monthly Budget Worksheet** starting on *page* 68 and the **Monthly Expense Record** starting on *page* 120 to help you use this section more efficiently. The design does allow planning from this form exclusively, however, the other worksheets are more comprehensive so there is less chance of overlooking any critical expenses.

If you have been using the Monthly Expense Record for *tracking* your daily spending, and have good records of all your fixed bills and general expenses, then those totals can easily be transferred to this worksheet. The Monthly Budget Worksheet allows more room for *projecting* your monthly plan of any upcoming bills and other unique expenses for the month.

Just a reminder, the Monthly Budget Worksheet is the beginning step if you don't have a history of expenses yet. This worksheet offers you a guideline to think about and project the many areas beyond the bills where money may be spent during each month.

Credit Cards

Once the basic living expenses are handled, it is time to calculate how much to pay toward the credit card balances. In an ideal world, the only credit card balances would be those that are paid off each month. Until that time arrives, use this worksheet to pay off your credit card balances as quickly as possible and not waste another dime on finance charges, late fees, and over-the-limit fees. The **Debt Payoff Record** (starting on *page* 104) can help you ultimately get on top of the debt situation.

If planning to make payments on the credit card debt is particularly difficult one month because of the low income and high fixed expenses, still try to find some way to pay the minimum due plus an extra ten dollars on each of the credit cards. This small additional amount will save you substantially over the long run.

During those months when a large sum of money is received, take this opportunity to pay down or off some or all of your credit card debt. Of course, a lot depends on the overall plan, your future income, and your future needs. Find a balance in this plan so you pay off enough of the credit card bill to save you significant finance charges and yet have enough funds to be prepared for future months of no income.

Major Periodic Expenses

The missing link in most budgets is the lack of planning for periodic expenses that show up throughout the year as quarterly, annual, or periodic expenses but are not part of the monthly picture.

The **Yearly Budget Worksheet** on *page* 52 will help you determine what periodic expenses exist and which ones are imperative to pay. If you have not yet completed this section, go ahead and review *pages* 50 and 51 for a suggested list of expenses that may apply to your situation right now. Add these totals to the worksheet under the appropriate monthly column.

Deposit to or Withdraw from Savings

Add your total income and total expenses under each month on this form. The idea here is to see how much money is left over or is short after taking care of all the basic needs outlined above. Once you can see that total amount in black and white, you can again take some constructive action. Depositing money into savings can be extremely satisfying after having a long stretch of debt and very little income.

For those surplus months, be sure to stash that excess money right away. If you have completed all the information for all months, it will be very apparent which months you will be needing to withdraw from savings to cover the expenses. The **Windfall Planner** on *page* 90 is another tool available for you in the event you unexpectedly receive a large sum of money.

There may still be situations where you can't predict when the next month will be a surplus or even an income month for you. In those cases, maximum savings is critical along with clear contingency plans as mentioned earlier. At some point, if this unpredictable income continues too long and erodes your savings, lifestyle, and personal well-being, you may want to reevaluate your work options or even where you now live.

Remember, when you have knowledge, you have more power to make decisions. Use this section as your road map to a more powerful financial future.

"It took us about seven months, but now we finally have a handle on our erratic income. There were times when we would go three months without any kind of income. In the beginning, it seemed like all we were doing was dodging phone calls and juggling promises. But then, by carefully tracking and planning our expenses over time and working closely with the creditors, we were able to work out how much we needed every month to run the household. When we finally did get paid we knew exactly what bills to pay, how much had to be covered, and what amount we needed to carry over into savings each time. What a difference this has made. We feel like we can breathe again!"

VARIABLE INCOME WORKSHEET

Income Source	Jan.	Feb.	Mar.	Apr.	May	June	July	Aug.	Sept.	Oct.	Nov.	Dec.	Total
Investment Income													
Commissions													
Bonus													
Business Income													
Consultant													
Reimbursement													
Freelance													
Royalty													
Other*													
TOTAL INCOME													

*Tax refund, cash gifts, inheritance, trust, gratuities, rental property, insurance settlement, property sale, affiliate website sales, etc.

BASIC MONTHLY HOUSEHOLD AND PERSONAL EXPENSES
(Refer to Monthly Budget Worksheet and Yearly Budget Worksheet for more comprehensive categories.)

Expense	Jan.	Feb.	Mar.	Apr.	May	June
Estimated Taxes						
Fixed: Mortgage/Rent						
Car Payment/Lease						
_____						
Loans						
_____						
Insurance						
_____						
_____						
Variable: Utilities						
Phones						
Groceries						
Gasoline						
_____						
_____						
Credit Cards: _____						
_____						
_____						
_____						
Major Periodic Expenses (*pg* 52)						
TOTAL EXPENSES						
Total Income (page 86)						
Difference						
Deposit into Savings*						
Withdraw from Savings						

*If extra funds are available this month, see the Windfall Planner on page 90.

BASIC MONTHLY HOUSEHOLD AND PERSONAL EXPENSES
(Refer to Monthly Budget Worksheet and Yearly Budget Worksheet for more comprehensive categories.)

Expense	July	Aug.	Sept.	Oct.	Nov.	Dec.
Estimated Taxes						
Fixed: Mortgage/Rent						
Car Payment/Lease						
_____						
Loans						
_____						
Insurance						
_____						
_____						
Variable: Utilities						
Phones						
Groceries						
Gasoline						
_____						
_____						
Credit Cards:						
_____						
_____						
_____						
Major Periodic Expenses: (*pg* 52)						
TOTAL EXPENSES						
Total Income (page 86)						
Difference						
Deposit into Savings*						
Withdraw from Savings						

*If extra funds are available this month, see the Windfall Planner on page 90.

Windfall Planner

Use this planner to outline a reasonable plan for prioritizing the distribution of lump sums of money, such as tax refunds, an inheritance, insurance settlements, company bonuses, sale of a home, cash gifts, royalties, auction or yard sales, and any other sources.

Be sure to have the expected or promised money actually in hand (in your bank) before making any payments or purchases. And, don't forget to handle any taxes that will be due up front if they have not yet been taken out.

For peace of mind and balance, consider paying portions to the *past, present,* and *future.* Pay off past debts, buy something on your wish list, and set aside money for future needs.

WINDFALL PLANNER

Date: _____

Source of Money: _____

Total Amount: _____

Possible Expense Item	Amount	or	Percent
Estimated Taxes to Put in Savings (If no taxes have been taken out.)	$ _____		_____ %
Catch Up on Payments Currently Behind	_____		_____
Back Taxes Still Due (federal, state, property)	_____		_____
Credit Card(s)—Pay Down or Off	_____		_____
Loan(s)—Pay Down or Off	_____		_____
Cover __ No. of Months of Living Expenses (Put this in savings.)	_____		_____
Stock Up on Household and/or Grocery Items	_____		_____
Upcoming Major Expense(s) (See Yearly Budget Worksheet on page 53.)	_____		_____
Reserve Savings Account (See Yearly Budget Worksheet on page 53.)	_____		_____
Emergency Savings Account	_____		_____
Home Improvement Project(s)	_____		_____
New Purchases	_____		_____
Investments/Retirement/College	_____		_____
Vacation/Travel/Trips/Fun money	_____		_____
Charitable Giving	_____		_____
Other _____	_____		_____
_____	_____		_____
_____	_____		_____
_____	_____		_____
_____	_____		_____
_____	_____		_____
_____	_____		_____
_____	_____		_____
_____	_____		_____
_____	_____		_____
_____	_____		_____
_____	_____		_____
_____	_____		_____
_____	_____		_____
_____	_____		_____
_____	_____		_____
_____	_____		_____
_____	_____		_____
_____	_____		_____
GRAND TOTAL	$ _____		_____ %

Multiple Sales
Monthly Planner

Whether you are an interior decorator in a home furnishing store, a REALTOR®, or software salesperson, if your income is based on commission, this **Multiple Sales Monthly Planner** is designed to help you get a handle on those ongoing monthly sales activities.

The goal is to have one place to list all your projected, pending, and closing sales for each month, and to keep the form open enough to allow for the many changes that occur throughout the month. This is another place it would be wise to use pencil.

Use this planner as an addendum to the forms you already use through your work. It also can be used to determine your variable income for each month, which you can record on the various worksheets in this workbook. This form is deliberately kept generic to address the unique needs of different sales environments.

You may need to alter code titles listed on the bottom of the planner, depending on the line of work you are in and, in some cases, they may not apply at all. The date as well as the amount for closing a sale or making a potential sale could be known or approximate; again, put down the information that works best for your needs.

Modify this planner as much as you need so it is a functional tool for you.

MULTIPLE SALES MONTHLY PLANNER

JANUARY

Code	Sales (Customer/Product)	Date	Amount

Notes:

Total Income $ _____

FEBRUARY

Code	Sales (Customer/Product)	Date	Amount

Notes:

Total Income $ _____

MARCH

Code	Sales (Customer/Product)	Date	Amount

Notes:

Total Income $ _____

APRIL

Code	Sales (Customer/Product)	Date	Amount

Notes:

Total Income $ _____

Code: F—Future Prospect/Project   L—Listing of a Sale   P—Pending Sale   S—Sold and Closed

MULTIPLE SALES MONTHLY PLANNER

MAY

Code	Sales (Customer/Product)	Date	Amount

Notes:

Total Income $ _____

JUNE

Code	Sales (Customer/Product)	Date	Amount

Notes:

Total Income $ _____

JULY

Code	Sales (Customer/Product)	Date	Amount

Notes:

Total Income $ _____

AUGUST

Code	Sales (Customer/Product)	Date	Amount

Notes:

Total Income $ _____

Code: F—Future Prospect/Project   L—Listing of a Sale   P—Pending Sale   S—Sold and Closed

MULTIPLE SALES MONTHLY PLANNER

SEPTEMBER

Code	Sales (Customer/Product)	Date	Amount

Notes:

Total Income $ _____

OCTOBER

Code	Sales (Customer/Product)	Date	Amount

Notes:

Total Income $ _____

NOVEMBER

Code	Sales (Customer/Product)	Date	Amount

Notes:

Total Income $ _____

DECEMBER

Code	Sales (Customer/Product)	Date	Amount

Notes:

Total Income $ _____

Code: F—Future Prospect/Project   L—Listing of a Sale   P—Pending Sale   S—Sold and Closed

Debt Payoff Record

"In two years' time we went from $16,000 debt to $2,000 (vehicles) and saved over $10,000. It took facing the numbers in the workbook, seeing what we spent every day, realizing how much money was going to finance charges, and getting out of our denial about debt. Now we still buy clothes and go on vacations. The difference is the planning and saving ahead of time."

When to Use this Worksheet

If you are beginning to get deep in debt or just need a better idea of how much you still owe on all your bills, such as medical expenses, car loan, finance company loan, credit cards, or department store cards, this worksheet is an important step for regaining financial control.

Staying organized is easier as well, as you now have a way to keep all your credit information in one simple place. You also can list the creditor's address and contact name, if you need this information frequently, in the blank space at the top or bottom of the page.

What to Include

The expenses to include are those you are unable to pay in full and must extend over a period of time (installment payments), such as automobile, home equity, student, or finance company loans; medical, legal, or family loans; IRS debt; and all credit card charges. This worksheet will clearly show you how much you have paid, what you still owe, and how much it is costing you to pay in installments. Remember, every penny you pay for finance charges is money you could have in your pocket for savings or vacations if the bills were paid in full.

How to Start

Start by filling in all the information at the top of the worksheet, such as the creditor's name and account number, for each debt you have. The "Total Balance Due" at the top gives you your starting figure so you can watch your progress. It will be helpful also to add the date somewhere on the top of this worksheet so you know your total beginning balance as of a specific date if you are not starting this form in January. Be sure to include the annual percentage rate (APR), which lets you know what interest rate you are paying.

As you make payments each month take time to actually look at your whole statement. I know the tendency is to zero in on the "Minimum Payment Due" block and ignore the rest. It's time to start paying attention to the other information on the statement like "New Balance," "Finance Charge," "Late Payment Fee," and "Over the Limit Fee." Granted, it's very difficult to acknowledge the whole picture, yet this is an important step and it's how you will begin to take charge and change your spending habits.

Fill in the "Amount Paid" and "Balance Due" for each month on this worksheet. The "Interest/Penalty" line is for all the finance charges and other fees. Just adding up that line across both pages will certainly get your attention each month.

Now really look at that statement and notice how much of the minimum payment you pay is for the finance charge and how much is actually payment toward the balance due. Amazing, isn't it? Now you see why it is taking so long to get out of debt.

Cost of Credit Card Purchases

Have you ever wondered how long it would take to pay off your credit card debt? Chart A shows an example of what you would pay if you only paid the minimum payment on a $2,000 balance and then what you would pay with just an extra 25 cents a day, or about $7.50 a month.

When comparing the different minimum *percent* payments on Chart A, the smaller minimum percent (2%) certainly looks more appealing when looking at the resulting lower minimum payment ($40) for Card A. Now notice how much it adds to the "Total Interest Cost" ($7,636) and the number of "Years to Payoff" needed (42 years) to eliminate the debt. You can see why it really does take "forever" to pay off your debt!

The remainder of Chart A on the right shows the savings by just adding 25 cents a day to your minimum payment or $7.50 a month. For that same example mentioned above, you would save $4,916 in interest, not to mention the 28 years of payments that would be eliminated.

Now let's see what a difference even smaller amounts can make. If you added only 10 cents a day extra (that's only about $3 a month) to a $5,000 credit card balance, which had a 2 percent minimum payment and a 17 percent interest rate, you would save $2,257 in interest!

Have I gotten your attention yet? The whole point is to increase those credit card payments above the minimum as much as you can. If you can pay the extra $100 or more each month, as many try to do, then go for it. If not, know that every effort you can make to pay some extra amount can have huge dividends for you in the long run.

One more note regarding minimum payments. With new federal guidelines, it may no longer be possible to make the bare minimum 2% of balance credit card payments as shown in Chart A and carry the balance "forever." Credit card companies have started doubling their minimum payments. On a new card, the minimum payment is probably now closer to 4% of the total balance due. Also, for those of you who have been diligently making your monthly payments, don't be fooled by the tempting "zero minimum payment due" on your statement. Continue to make a minimum payment every month and start using at least 4% of the current balance due as a base amount. Like everything else related to credit cards, be sure to monitor your cards and all the insert notices carefully. These companies can and often do change the rules anytime, including the annual percentage rate (APR) and minimum payment due.

Charts B and C are designed to encourage you and show you it is possible to be debt free. In Chart B on *page* 98, an arbitrary 14 percent average is used for total debt, which could be a consolidation loan. My goal is to give you a sense of possibility. Find your total debt due in the left-hand column and then pick the amount you can afford each month, or the number of years you want to set as your goal to be debt free, in the columns to the right. Once you know that figure, you can start to do whatever it takes to make that monthly payment happen and get your debt paid off.

Let's say your goal is to be debt free in three or five years. Use Chart C on page 101 to find your interest rate and then pick your payments according to the three- or five-year plans and total debt due.

There are many books on the market, software packages, and websites available to help you learn how to reduce your debt. These charts are provided merely as a sampling to motivate you to find the resources you need.

The information in these charts is from the authors of *Slash Your Debt: Save Money and Secure Your Future*. Gerri Detweiler, Marc Eisenson, and Nancy Castleman have done a fantastic job of bringing together some of the most comprehensive, easy-to-read, and practical tips, examples, resources, and strategies I have seen. They provide nearly a dozen tables showing you how to reduce your credit card and mortgage debt (see *www.goodadvicepress.com*).

CHART A: THE COST OF CREDIT CARD PURCHASES
BALANCE $2,000

	TOTAL COST WHEN PAYING ONLY THE MINIMUM PAYMENT					SAVINGS WHEN ADDING AN EXTRA $.25/DAY TO PAYMENT		
CARD	Interest Rate	Minimum Percent Payment	Minimum Payment	Total Interest Cost	YEARS* to Payoff	Interest Paid after Extra $.25/Day	Total Interest Saved	YEARS* Saved by Extra $.25/Day
CARD A	19.8 %	2 %	$40	$7,636	42	$2,720	$4,916	28
CARD B	19.8	2.78	56	2,585	17	1,557	1,029	8
CARD C	12.5	2	40	1,840	18	1,071	769	8
CARD D	8.25	3	60	542	10	400	142	3

*This information was in months, which was rounded up to make the extra year.

Source: *The Banker's Secret Credit Card Software*. This program makes it easy to crunch the numbers for your own credit cards, so you can see how much you can save by making payments greater than the required minimums. (*www.goodadvicepress.com*)

CHART B: HOW SOON CAN YOU BE DEBT FREE?

The following figures are based on a debt with an average 14 percent interest rate.

If you want your debt paid off in the following years, see the chart below to find out how much your monthly payment would be to reach your debt-free goal.

Total Debt Due	1 Yr.	2 Yrs.	3 Yrs.	4 Yrs.	5 Yrs.	6 Yrs.	7 Yrs.	8 Yrs.	9 Yrs.	10 Yrs.
$ 3,000	$ 270	$ 144	$ 103	$ 82	$ 70	$ 62	$ 56	$ 52	$ 49	$ 47
5,000	449	240	171	137	116	103	94	87	82	78
10,000	898	480	342	273	233	206	187	174	163	155
15,000	1,347	720	513	410	349	309	281	261	245	233
20,000	1,796	960	684	547	465	412	375	347	327	311
25,000	2,245	1,200	854	683	582	515	469	434	408	388
30,000	2,694	1,440	1,025	820	698	618	562	521	490	466
35,000	3,143	1,680	1,196	956	814	721	656	608	572	543
40,000	3,591	1,921	1,367	1,093	931	824	750	695	653	621
45,000	4,040	2,161	1,538	1,230	1,047	927	843	782	735	699
50,000	4,489	2,401	1,709	1,366	1,163	1,030	937	869	817	776
75,000	6,734	3,601	2,563	2,049	1,745	1,545	1,406	1,303	1,225	1,165

Total Monthly Payment

Getting Out of Debt

After you pay off one debt, apply that same payment amount to another debt, preferably one with the highest interest, to shorten the term of that debt. An exception is if you have a smaller debt (even those with a lower interest rate) and you need the psychological satisfaction of making progress, then pay off that debt as soon as you can. As you continue to apply payments from paid-off debt to remaining debt, you will start to see how soon and how much of your total debt will be paid off in one or a few years.

By the following year, through the conscientious use of the worksheets in this workbook, you no longer may need this worksheet. Hurrah! As one reader put it, "This Debt Payoff Record form makes the whole workbook worth hugging a thousand times!"

Want Your Credit Card Paid Off in 11 Months?

If you have 3 factors in place, you can pay off any credit card balance in 11 months.

- The interest rate is less than 20%
- You pay 10% of the current balance and make that same payment every single month.
- No additional charging on your credit card

For example, if your balance is $5000, you would pay $500 every single month. If your balance was $7500, you would pay $750 every month. The total amount of finance charge you are paying overall will vary depending on the interest rate, but the 11 months to pay off the total balance will stay the same provided your interest rate is under 20%.

Monthly Payment Needed to be Debt Free in 11 Months				
Credit Card	**Total Debt**	**× 10%**	**=**	**Monthly Payment**
MasterCard	$5000	× 10%	=	$500
_____	$_____	× 10%	=	$_____
_____	$_____	× 10%	=	$_____
_____	$_____	× 10%	=	$_____

How Long will it take to Pay Off your Credit Card?
(Assuming you have a current 0% rate card)

If you are looking for a quick snapshot of the length of time needed to pay off your credit cards based on how much you can pay each month, you can do the following exercise.

Credit Card	Total Debt	÷	Monthly Payment	=	Months to Pay Off
Visa	$5000	÷	$150	=	33 months (2 yrs and 9 months)
_____	$_____	÷	$_____	=	_____ months
_____	$_____	÷	$_____	=	_____ months
_____	$_____	÷	$_____	=	_____ months

If your credit cards do have interest rates under 20%, depending on the interest rate and the percent of balance you are paying, tack on another 3–11 months for a *rough estimate* of how long it will take you to pay off each card. Remember, the higher the interest rate and the lower the payment, the more months it will take to pay off. **The key is the constant monthly payment of the same amount regardless of the changing balance due.**

Remember, these are *very general* guidelines to give you a quick snapshot of an estimate. For much more accurate information which will factor in the compounding aspect of interest rates, use a business calculator. If you have online access, the simplest solution is to go to any of the following online calculators or your own favorite calculator websites, and plug in your balance due, interest rate, and monthly payments or percent of balance you want to pay:

- cgi.money.cnn.com/tools/debtplanner/debtplanner.jsp
- www.bankrate.com/brm/calc/creditcardpay.asp
- www.choosetosave.org/calculators/
- www1.cardtrak.com/cardtrak/calc/payment.amp
- www.cardratings.com/creditcarddebtcalc.html

Getting Control of your Finances

When you reach the point where you become a wise and responsible consumer and you use credit to your advantage only as a means of using someone else's money and can pay the bill in full when it is due, you will know you truly have control of your finances! You also will have much greater peace of mind.

Making Money Instead of Spending Money

"Those who understand interest collect it, and those who don't pay it."

— William H. Stone

Once you have gotten into the habit of making payments and applying extra money from paid-off debt to reducing the remaining debt, you will have acquired a great skill. When your debts are paid off, you can continue the payment schedule, only this time putting money into your savings and investments. All that money that was used to pay off the debt-plus-interest and penalty charges now can go toward your savings for you. Instead of spending money, you actually will be making money on the same payment amounts.

CHART C: PICK A MONTHLY PAYMENT TO PAY YOUR DEBT OFF IN THREE TO FIVE YEARS								
Total Debt Due	Years	Consolidation Loan Rate						
		8%	9%	10%	11%	12%	13%	14%
$ 5,000	3	$ 157	$ 159	$ 161	$ 164	$ 166	$ 168	$ 171
	5	101	104	106	109	111	114	116
7,500	3	235	239	242	246	249	253	256
	5	152	156	159	163	167	171	175
10,000	3	313	318	323	327	332	337	342
	5	203	208	212	217	222	228	233
12,500	3	392	398	403	409	415	421	427
	5	253	259	266	272	278	284	291
15,000	3	470	477	484	491	498	505	513
	5	304	311	319	326	334	341	349
17,500	3	548	557	565	573	581	590	598
	5	355	363	372	381	389	398	407
20,000	3	627	636	645	655	664	674	684
	5	406	415	425	435	445	455	465
25,000	3	783	795	807	818	830	842	854
	5	507	519	531	544	556	569	582
30,000	3	940	954	968	982	996	1,011	1,025
	5	608	623	637	652	667	683	698
35,000	3	1,097	1,113	1,129	1,146	1,163	1,179	1,196
	5	710	727	744	761	779	796	814
40,000	3	1,253	1,272	1,291	1,310	1,329	1,348	1,367
	5	811	830	850	870	890	910	931
45,000	3	1,410	1,431	1,452	1,473	1,495	1,516	1,538
	5	912	934	956	978	1,001	1,024	1,047
50,000	3	1,567	1,590	1,613	1,637	1,661	1,685	1,709
	5	1,014	1,038	1,062	1,087	1,112	1,138	1,163

Source: This table is reprinted with permission from *Slash Your Debt: Save Money & Secure Your Future* (2001, Financial Literacy Center, *www.goodadvicepress.com*).

Let's see what kind of money you could be making. Chart D gives you an idea of just how much money. Using the same $2,000 credit card balance example from Chart A, look what can happen if you *invested* $2,000 at 10 percent instead of *spending* $2,000 at 19.8 percent. Rather than paying off the $2,000 debt for 42 years and *paying* $7,636 in interest, you would be *earning* $131,072 (compounded monthly) in 40 years. Not bad for only a $2,000 investment.

CHART D: $2,000 One-Time Investment—No Annual Contributions			
Years	**6%**	**10%**	**14%**
10	$ 3,639	$ 5,414	$ 8,045
20	6,620	14,656	32,361
30	12,045	39,675	130,169
40	24,702	131,072	691,672

Calculations were compounded monthly.

Source: These figures were calculated by Marc Eisenson of *www.goodadvicepress. com*, author of *The Banker's Secret*, and coauthor of *Slash Your Debt: Save Money & Secure Your Future* and *Invest in Yourself: Six Secrets to a Rich Life*.

Fortunately, there are now numerous website resources and calculators for finding and evaluating investments and higher returns. By researching and finding higher investment returns, you can see the payoff for investing over 10 to 40 years.

Best of all, not only will you have assets instead of debts, you will feel encouraged, excited, and confident about your financial skills.

"Thank you for getting us jump-started! It was most helpful to see which debts to focus on so we could prioritize our debt-payoff plan. We buckled down to really change and pay attention to our spending, and now we are so inspired to pay off our final debts that we have hired a financial planner to help us invest our new-found money."

GETTING ONLINE HELP

As of this printing, there are numerous Internet-based nonprofit organizations and "for-profit" companies and practitioners providing financial information, services, counseling (in person, by phone, or on the Internet), coaching, and support.

Unfortunately, over the years many unscrupulous debt management firms have cropped up that take advantage of the national high-debt situation and offer quick-fix solutions. These firms manage to get nonprofit status, which confuses the consumer even more because he or she does not know how to distinguish a legitimate agency from an abusive one.

Legitimate credit counseling firms will meet or talk with their clients, review their finances, and recommend a budget and/or debt payment plan. Fees are generally nominal or there are none at all. If you initially see that the service is free but later learn there is a "donation cost" or other significant expense for every service, consider this a warning sign.

Rather than include an exhaustive, ever-changing list of organizations and services, I am recommending you do a search on *www.google.com* or any other favorite search engine. Start with "financial counseling" or "debt management" for your key word search.

Below are two national organizations with an established history:

National Foundation for Credit Counseling (NFCC)
www.nfcc.org; 800-388-2227

NFCC is the nation's oldest, largest, and longest-serving nonprofit credit counseling network, setting the national standard for quality credit counseling, debt reduction services, and education for financial wellness. Member agencies around the country, often known as the Consumer Credit Counseling Service (CCCS) or other names, can be identified by the NFCC member seal. Their seal signifies high standards for agency accreditation, counselor certification, and policies that ensure confidential services. Their programs are designed to help you make one payment, get debt paid off early, and reduce the amount of monthly creditor payments, often by negotiating for reduced or eliminated finance charges and other fees.

Association for Financial Counseling and Planning Education (AFCPE)
www.afcpe.org; 614-485-9650

AFCPE is a professional organization that supports and promotes the field of financial counseling and planning education. The membership consists of university and Cooperative Extension educators, military financial counselors, private practitioners, and interest organization and government officials.

Getting help from a Financial Counselor (whether through an organization or privately) can be invaluable to help you improve your financial situation and your emotional and mental state. Ask about their background training and accreditation. If possible, find someone who is certified as an Accredited Financial Counselor (AFC) through AFCPE.

DEBT PAYOFF RECORD

	Loans				Credits Cards	
CREDITOR						
Account Number						
Total Balance Due						
Phone Number						
Interest Rate (APR)						
January						
Amount Paid						
Interest/Penalty						
Balance Due						
February						
Amount Paid						
Interest/Penalty						
Balance Due						
March						
Amount Paid						
Interest/Penalty						
Balance Due						
April						
Amount Paid						
Interest/Penalty						
Balance Due						
May						
Amount Paid						
Interest/Penalty						
Balance Due						
June						
Amount Paid						
Interest/Penalty						
Balance Due						
July						
Amount Paid						
Interest/Penalty						
Balance Due						
August						
Amount Paid						
Interest/Penalty						
Balance Due						
September						
Amount Paid						
Interest/Penalty						
Balance Due						
October						
Amount Paid						
Interest/Penalty						
Balance Due						
November						
Amount Paid						
Interest/Penalty						
Balance Due						
December						
Amount Paid						
Interest/Penalty						
Balance Due						
Balance Due						

DEBT PAYOFF RECORD

Other (Medical, Legal, Personal, etc.)						Total

Debt Repayment Worksheet

Once you have completed the top part of the **Debt Payoff Record** on *pages 104–105* and outlined all of your debt, it may be overwhelming to stop and see the total amount of debt to be paid off. If you are in a situation where there is not enough disposable money each month to even pay the monthly minimums, and you are determined to pay back your debt in full, know that there is a solution.

The **Debt Repayment Worksheet** is provided to help when you are *in a very tight financial situation and choose not to declare bankruptcy or use the services of any nonprofit credit counseling agency.* This approach will take time and patience. The payoff, however, will be preservation of your personal and financial integrity.

This repayment concept has been discussed and outlined very thoroughly in Jerrold Mundis's *How to Get Out of Debt, Stay Out of Debt and Live Prosperously* and Dave Ramsey's *The Financial PeacePlanner* books. The **Debt Repayment Worksheet** summarizes how to work out a fair share repayment plan for all of your creditors using what disposable money you have available to pay off your debt.

How to Use this Worksheet

First, fill out your **Monthly Budget Worksheet** (starting on *page 68*), so you know exactly how much your monthly bills and expenses are. Next, determine how much money you can use to pay toward your debt. With this figure and your total balances from the **Debt Payoff Record** beginning on page 104, we will work out each creditor's percentage and the amount of money you have available for paying them.

To make this method work, there are four things you need to do:

1. Contact each creditor and explain your plan by including a copy of your budget, the first payment check, and this outline of debt repayment.
2. Stay honest and stick to your commitment religiously, and make every one of these monthly payments on time.
3. Track and manage your spending diligently.
4. Do not incur any new debt.

It also doesn't hurt to *pray* in your own way!

During this repayment period, it also will be important to find ways to raise some extra cash to pay toward your debt or to cover the surprise incidentals that come up, whether through selling items, holding yard sales, working overtime, or getting part-time work. Apply any extra money from gifts, rebates, or refunds toward this debt. In the future you will have the opportunity again to treat yourself with that gift money. For now you are trading a piece of furniture or jewelry for some peace of mind.

If your creditors resist the nominal payment amounts (for example, they are asking for payments of $100 and you are sending $35), remind them you are doing this to avoid bankruptcy and persist with your program and keep making payments. Hold the goal of being debt free and keep knowing that you can pay off your debt slowly and methodically. Continue to explain and show your plan and follow through with it.

You can't be forced to pay money you do not have. This system will give you the strength to resist aggressive creditors. If you pay more than planned to one aggressive creditor, the whole repayment plan will go out of balance and you will be back in the familiar discouraging debt cycle again.

Keep in mind this financial condition will eventually pass. Amazingly, you will find that these initial small amounts of payments start to increase as you slowly begin to pay off debt and work with a program. As each creditor gets paid in full over time, *recalculate the balance due and the total combined debt.* Increase your payments accordingly, and you will start to see those balances go down. Stop and realize that you are now getting *out of debt* instead of into debt, and notice how you are starting to regain a solid sense of control in your life once again.

As Winston Churchill once said: "Never, never, never give up!"

DEBT REPAYMENT WORKSHEET

Step 1 Disposable Income*

Total Amount of Disposable Income Available to Pay Off Debt: $_____
(Calculate your budget on the **Monthly Budget Worksheet** beginning on page 68.)
The more you owe a creditor, the more money and higher percent you will pay them
from your Disposable Income.

Step 2 Total Combined Debt**

Total Amount of All Debt Combined: $_____
(Transfer the total from the **Debt Payoff Record** beginning on page 104.)

Step 3 New Payment

List below the total balances you owe each creditor listed on the **Debt Payoff Record** on *page* 105.
Start with the smallest balance and then follow the formula below to determine the new payment for
each creditor.

Creditor	Balance Due	÷	Total** Combined Debt	=	Share Percent (of Total Combined Debt)	×	Disposable* Income		New Payment
Dentist	$500	÷	$11,500	=	4.3%	×	$700	=	$30.43
Visa	$1,500	÷	$11,500	=	13%	×	$700	=	$91.30
_____	_____		_____		_____		_____		_____
_____	_____		_____		_____		_____		_____
_____	_____		_____		_____		_____		_____
_____	_____		_____		_____		_____		_____
_____	_____		_____		_____		_____		_____
_____	_____		_____		_____		_____		_____
_____	_____		_____		_____		_____		_____
_____	_____		_____		_____		_____		_____
_____	_____		_____		_____		_____		_____
_____	_____		_____		_____		_____		_____
_____	_____		_____		_____		_____		_____
_____	_____		_____		_____		_____		_____
_____	_____		_____		_____		_____		_____

Credit Card Purchase Record

To avoid a shocking bill at the end of the month, keep careful track of your credit card charges. This way, you can anticipate what the bill will be and prepare for it by making the appropriate adjustments in your spending and your planning.

By knowing the status of your charges at all times, you become much more selective and careful about impulse charging. When you reach this point, you know that you have learned how to keep from getting overextended and have taken one more step toward controlling your finances.

How to Use this Chart

First find out and enter the "Billing Cycle Closing Date." ① Call each credit card company and ask them what this date is for your account. By knowing this information, you can manage your charges and payments more proactively instead of unconsciously. Then record all charges ② made during the month until that date so you know which purchases will be included on that month's upcoming bill. Purchases charged after that closing date should be entered in the next month's column (the month for which you actually will be billed). Jot down in the corner the date you made the charge. ③

Remember, this chart is flexible. If you use different cards frequently, use the duplicate chart that follows. Draw one or two lines across both pages to create new sections for different cards. You also can carry an extra check register with you to record your charges for other cards. Make the chart work for you!

CREDIT CARD PURCHASE RECORD   SAMPLE

JAN.		FEB.		MAR.		APR.		MAY		JUNE	
Billing Cycle Closing Date: ① _____		_____		_____		_____		_____		_____	
Purchase	Amount	Purchase	Amount	Purchase	Amount	Purchase	Amount	Purchase	Amount	Purchase	Amount
③ 3/gas ②	14.91										
7/Shoes	20.82										
Total											

ONLINE/ELECTRONIC CONNECTION TO *THE BUDGET KIT*

Online Bill Payments

If you don't want to list your charges on this worksheet, you can register online at your credit card company's website and see your current charges and balance due. As you fill in the "Installment" blanks of the **Monthly Budget Worksheet** to plan out your bills, you will know exactly how much to anticipate for your credit card payments. When your bill arrives, you can still pay by check or pay the bill directly online from your checking account, using either the credit card website or your bank's website.

Online Budget Programs

Coordinating credit card charges with a monthly budget accurately and effectively is probably one of the more challenging steps depending on your online budget program, credit card debt situation, and level of sophistication. Even the manual approach to this process gets confusing for many people. See if your online budget program has a way to link a credit card charge in a particular category with the same category in your outlined budget for the month and then has a way to plan the payment. Not all programs are designed to coordinate this process.

The more popular online budget programs like Mvelopes® Personal, Microsoft Money, and Quicken Personal Products will have well designed systems for virtually coordinating the credit card charges, with the monthly budget and then include a virtual transfer for the payment plan. If you are a heavy credit card user, be sure this feature is offered with the online program you are using and is easy to use.

CREDIT CARD PURCHASE RECORD

JAN.		FEB.		MAR.		APR.		MAY		JUNE	
Billing Cycle Closing Date: _____		_____		_____		_____		_____		_____	
Purchase	Amount	Purchase	Amount	Purchase	Amount	Purchase	Amount	Purchase	Amount	Purchase	Amount
Total											

CREDIT CARD PURCHASE RECORD

JULY		AUG.		SEPT.		OCT.		NOV.		DEC.	
Billing Cycle Closing Date: _____		_____		_____		_____		_____		_____	
Purchase	Amount	Purchase	Amount	Purchase	Amount	Purchase	Amount	Purchase	Amount	Purchase	Amount
Total											

Monthly Expense Record

Sometimes it takes the black-and-white approach to get someone's attention. Connie started using the workbook to track expenses and plan ahead when she and her husband knew they would be retiring in a few years. Her husband was staggered when he saw the expenses they both spent for six months. He was finally ready to sit down and outline and plan the finances together with Connie. They also successfully started saving for their travel plans. The workbook became an effective communication tool—a way for getting out of the dream world and back into reality.

Finding Out Where All the Money Goes

How many times have you asked yourself "Where did all the money go?" Even keeping detailed records in the check register or reviewing the bank statements and credit card statements doesn't always give a clear answer to that question. With these worksheets and with some firm self-discipline, you will easily and very graphically know in a more organized way exactly where all your money has gone as well as how much money has come in.

Begin by picking a time every day to jot down all the spending for that day. Some people like to carry a small notebook or use their PDA to record all their daily cash in a more organized way. Others carry this workbook or these sheets in their car, backpack, or briefcase and record as they go. With practice and determination, you will develop the habit of regularly recording all *cash, debits, checks,* and *charged* expenses. At first this may seem time-consuming and uncomfortable. However, once you get past the 21-day marker for creating a new habit, you will notice that your recording literally takes only minutes a day.

Be patient with yourself and the results. The first month or two your numbers may not be perfect, but the habit is being developed and information is emerging. By the third month or earlier you will be amazed at the results and the shift in your attitude.

By using this worksheet, you will have a total multi-sensory impact subconsciously, on your spending. Kinesthetically, you are manually writing down each expense. Recording daily versus recording a basketful of receipts at the end of each week or month, will give you more valuable input than you realize. Visually, you are taking the information in and noticing all the other entries in the column above. Subconsciously, you are starting to note all the money spent to date and probably thinking you want to cut back. And then when you start talking to your partner or to yourself about the expenses, you are engaging the auditory senses. All of these senses combined are changing the way you manage and handle your money.

Ultimately your payoff will be the sense of control you have over your finances and finally being aware of your overall spending. Many people insist that once they began tracking their spending, they started spending less and saving more.

Recording cash spent is important. Every time you write a check for cash or use the automated teller machine (ATM), write down where you actually spend that cash. Itemizing all the cash provides more valuable information for you than just recording "$50 cash" or "misc." six times as an expense and not really knowing how it was spent or "where the money went."

Debit cards and ATMs as conveniences can be either a blessing or a curse depending on how you use them. After months of total chaos and overdraft charges in the checking account, one couple worked out their monthly budget to determine exactly how much cash was needed each week. On Mondays Joe gets his lump cash and knows it has to cover his gas, coffee, meals, snacks, and all other incidentals for the week. Ginny sticks with the check-book. Both are relieved to finally always know their current balance in the checkbook.

If you seem to have more month than money most of the time, remember your choices. You can reduce, postpone, modify, or eliminate your spending. If you are not sure where to begin, a review of these filled-out worksheets will quickly show you which optional categories to start with. Maybe you need to do more of your own home or car repairs, be more energy-conscious, eat out less, take your lunch and beverages to work, cut back on gifts, start carpooling, or do whatever fits your abilities and interests. When you do cut back, the results will be noticed immediately.

As you work with these worksheets, modify them to fit your unique life-style. The expense categories, net income, savings, investment, and retirement sections serve as guidelines to set up your own system.

If you have tax-deductible expenses, note them here. If you want all you tax records kept together, you can use the handy **Tax-Deductible Expense Record** in Part Three.

You will notice the emphasis on *net income*, not on gross income, throughout this workbook. The idea is to deal only with actual money and not record more information than you need to. The gross income information is usually on your check stubs. If you need to keep a record of your taxes, FICA, retirement savings, and other deductions, you can use the "End-of-the-Year Tax Information" section on the bottom of the **Summary-for-the-Year Record** worksheet following these monthly expense pages.

"I like using a color code like a highlighter or some key symbols to designate where the money came from to pay for certain expenses. It helps me know when I used money from our reserve account or household savings account. That way I feel I'm working with a plan and can see how the extra expenses are planned and covered."

THE ONLINE/ELECTRONIC CONNECTION TO *THE BUDGET KIT*

Electronic Tracking Systems

The **Monthly Expense Record** is actually a very effective tool to use as a guideline for setting up any electronic tracking system and understanding the basic concept behind the tracking. Over the years, people have called telling me how they preferred the organization and the categories from this worksheet to the categories in the personal finance software package they were using. Instead of organizing the spending categories alphabetically, this worksheet was designed around the actual spending styles of thousands of readers and clients.

Whether you use your own created worksheet, a personal finance software program like Quicken Deluxe, Microsoft Money, or AceMoney or an online budget system, you can utilize the most helpful aspects of this worksheet as you transition over to electronic tracking.

The key with any system is interacting directly with all your spending transactions. This will keep you from going into automatic pilot with your daily spending and help you stay more in touch with your overall financial situation.

To review different personal finance software programs, do a Google search for "personal finance software review" or check out *personal-finance-software-review.toptenreviews.com*.

For the above mentioned software, see

quicken.intuit.com

www.microsoft.com/money

www.mechcad.net/products/acemoney

Monthly Expense Record Worksheet on Excel

If you're not quite ready to move over to a total personal finance software program or online budget system just yet, but do feel comfortable using Excel, there is another option. The worksheets on the following pages are part of the core worksheets available on Excel. These are available at *http://moneytracker. com/books-TheBudgetKitExcel.htm*. The worksheets look exactly the same way on the screen as on these pages and have the added convenience of doing all the calculations for you. There are separate tabs on the bottom for every month and then a Summary for the Year that is automatically totaling every time you enter an expense. Here again, I do recommend starting out manually with the workbook first for a month or so because of the advantages mentioned earlier.

MONTHLY EXPENSE RECORD

Balance Forward from Last Month:

Cash $37.00   Checking $62.00   Savings $11,796.45

NET INCOME

SALARY/COMMISSIONS	Chris	Kim	TOTAL
	896.00		
		1,407.43	
	883.00		
		1,407.43	
	TOTAL INCOME		4,593.86

OTHER		
Yard Sale—273		273.00
TOTAL INCOME		4,866.86

SAVINGS

(Describe)	
Reserve (used other $257 this month)	750.00
Goals	75.00
Emergency	215.00
TOTAL SAVINGS	1,040.00

INVESTMENTS/RETIREMENT

(See Payroll Deduction)	
TOTAL INVESTMENTS	

	FOOD groceries	fast food / dining out / school lunches	tobacco / alcohol / snacks / beverages / water	HOUSEHOLD cleaner / mainten. / house / yard / pool	appliances / furniture / furnishings / supplies	postage / ATM fees / bank chg. / misc.	interest / taxes	gas	TRANSPORTATION auto mainten. / wash / license	taxi / transit / tolls / parking	PERSONAL clothing / alterations / dry clean. / laundry / shoe care	toiletries / cosmetics / hair / nails / massage	HEALTH doctor / dentist / vision / medicine / vitamins	personal growth / therapy
W1	40.00	15.00						13.92						
2		7.50		20.34	33.67									
3	35.94							9.35				25.00		65.30
4			15.31						24.73		21.82		10.20	
5		28.98												
6			5.10											
7	44.48		6.05								15.03			
W8													33.68	
9	67.10	7.50				29.00					43.98			
10								14.79						
11	7.25	14.22										19.00		
12			4.95										13.00	
13			5.10	14.76					6.95					
14			6.05											
W15	10.53											21.46		
16		12.35						10.45			20.80			
17														
18	28.55	7.50	5.10											
19												25.00		
20	9.57										13.57			
21					23.00									65.30
W22		11.08						15.65						
23				10.45										
24														
25	149.73													
26		7.50	4.95					9.35			15.41			
27						8.50								
28	19.52													
29				4.31										
30	67.10	27.34						19.95						
31	8.59													
Total	458.36	127.89	63.69	49.86	56.67	37.50	—	93.46	31.68	—	130.41	90.46	56.88	130.60
Budget	450	125	50	55	55	35		100	4.5		125	95	65	130.60
Difference	8.36	<2.89>	<13.69>	5.14	<1.67>	<2.50>		6.54	13.32		<5.41>	4.54	8.12	—

MONTHLY EXPENSE RECORD

FIXED EXPENSES

Monthly	Amount	Monthly	Amount
Mortgage/Rent	784.00	Insurance:	
Assn. Fee		House/Apt	
Gas/Fuel	73.00	Auto	
Electricity	89.00	Life	54.00
Water/Refuse		Health (Payroll ded.)	
Garbage/Sewer		Dental	
Telephone	53.21	Disability	
Cellular Phone			
Cable/Satellite	35.00	Storage	75.00
Internet			
Child Support			
Spousal Support			
Health Club			
TOTAL	1,034.21	**TOTAL**	129.00

INSTALLMENT EXPENSES

Loans/Credit Cards	Amount
Visa	75.00
MC	50.00
Student Loan	167.00
Car Payment	291.00
TOTAL	583.00

TOTAL EXPENSES

Total Fixed Expenses	1,163.21
Total Installment Expenses	583.00
Total Monthly Expenses from Below	1,932.05
GRAND TOTAL	3,678.26

+ Savings (1,040.00) = $4,718.26

	RECREATION		EDUCATION		FAMILY			GENERAL					
vacation trips	entertain. DVD movie music parties	lottery sports hobbies lessons clubs	computer upgrades software supplies service	seminar workshop tuition supplies	newspaper books magazines games	elder care child care sitter tutor	infant exp. allowance school exp. toys arcades	pet vet supplies services	gifts cards flowers	charitable contribut. church temple	work expense dues	prof. services legal CPA investment	other (explanation)
1							10.00			50.00			
2	3.21								40.00				
3													
4													
5							10.00						
6													
7										50.00			
8							3.57						
9		19.22											
10									3.59				
11					15.22								
12							10.00						
13										50.00			
14									10.56				
15							15.98						
16													
17	15.04												
18					23.78		10.00						
19									2.60	50.00			
20													
21													
22					39.00								
23							4.98						
24													
25										40.00			
26													
27							10.00						
28	57.84												
29													
30													
31										60.00			
Total	76.09	19.22	—	—	78.00	—	74.53	—	56.75	300.00	—	—	—
Budget	75	25	25		75		70		50	300			
Difference	<1.09>	5.78	25		<3>		4.53		<6.75>	—			

MONTHLY EXPENSE RECORD

NET INCOME			
			TOTAL
SALARY/COMMISSIONS			
TOTAL INCOME			
OTHER			
TOTAL INCOME			

SAVINGS	
(Describe)	
TOTAL SAVINGS	

INVESTMENTS/RETIREMENT	
TOTAL INVESTMENTS	

	FOOD		HOUSEHOLD						TRANSPORTATION			PERSONAL		HEALTH	
	groceries	fast food / dining out / school / lunches	tobacco / alcohol / snacks / beverages / water	cleaner / mainten. / house / yard / pool	appliances / furniture / furnishings / supplies	postage / ATM fees / bank chg. / misc.	interest / taxes		gas	auto / mainten. / wash / license	taxi / transit / tolls / parking	clothing / alterations / dry clean. / laundry / shoe care	toiletries / cosmetics / hair / nails / massage	doctor / dentist / vision / medicine / vitamins	personal / growth / therapy
W E E K 1	1														
	2														
	3														
	4														
	5														
	6														
	7														
W E E K 2	8														
	9														
	10														
	11														
	12														
	13														
	14														
W E E K 3	15														
	16														
	17														
	18														
	19														
	20														
	21														
W E E K 4	22														
	23														
	24														
	25														
	26														
	27														
	28														
	29														
	30														
	31														
	Total														
	Budget														
	Difference														

MONTHLY EXPENSE RECORD

FIXED EXPENSES

Monthly	Amount	Monthly	Amount
Mortgage/Rent		Insurance:	
Assn. Fee		House/Apt	
Gas/Fuel		Auto	
Electricity		Life	
Water/Refuse		Health	
Garbage/Sewer		Dental	
Telephone		Disability	
Cellular Phone			
Cable/Satellite			
Internet			
Child Support			
Spousal Support			
Health Club			
TOTAL		**TOTAL**	

INSTALLMENT EXPENSES

Loans/Credit Cards	Amount
TOTAL	

TOTAL EXPENSES

Total Fixed Expenses	
Total Installment Expenses	
Total Monthly Expenses from Below	
GRAND TOTAL	

	RECREATION			EDUCATION			FAMILY				GENERAL					
vacation trips	entertain. video movie music parties	lottery sports hobbies lessons clubs	computer upgrades software supplies service	seminar workshop tuition supplies	newspaper books magazines games	elder care child care sitter tutor	infant exp. allowance school exp. toys arcades	pet vet supplies services		gifts cards flowers	charitable contribut. church temple	work expense dues	prof. services legal CPA investment	other (explanation)
1														
2														
3														
4														
5														
6														
7														
8														
9														
10														
11														
12														
13														
14														
15														
16														
17														
18														
19														
20														
21														
22														
23														
24														
25														
26														
27														
28														
29														
30														
31														
Total														
Budget														
Difference														

MONTHLY EXPENSE RECORD

Balance Forward from Last Month:

Cash _____ Checking _____ Savings _____

NET INCOME			TOTAL
SALARY/COMMISSIONS			
TOTAL INCOME			
OTHER			
TOTAL INCOME			

SAVINGS	
(Describe)	
TOTAL SAVINGS	

INVESTMENTS/RETIREMENT	
TOTAL INVESTMENTS	

		FOOD		HOUSEHOLD					TRANSPORTATION			PERSONAL		HEALTH	
		groceries	fast food dining out school lunches	tobacco alcohol snacks beverages water	cleaner mainten. house yard pool	appliances furniture furnishings supplies	postage ATM fees bank chg. misc.	interest taxes	gas	auto mainten. wash license	taxi transit tolls parking	clothing alterations dry clean. laundry shoe care	toiletries cosmetics hair nails massage	doctor dentist vision medicine vitamins	personal growth therapy
W	1														
E	2														
E	3														
K	4														
	5														
1	6														
	7														
W	8														
E	9														
E	10														
K	11														
	12														
2	13														
	14														
W	15														
E	16														
E	17														
K	18														
	19														
3	20														
	21														
W	22														
E	23														
E	24														
K	25														
	26														
4	27														
	28														
	29														
	30														
	31														
	Total														
	Budget														
	Difference														

MONTHLY EXPENSE RECORD

FIXED EXPENSES			
Monthly	Amount	Monthly	Amount
Mortgage/Rent		Insurance:	
Assn. Fee		House/Apt	
Gas/Fuel		Auto	
Electricity		Life	
Water/Refuse		Health	
Garbage/Sewer		Dental	
Telephone		Disability	
Cellular Phone			
Cable/Satellite			
Internet			
Child Support			
Spousal Support			
Health Club			
TOTAL		TOTAL	

INSTALLMENT EXPENSES	
Loans/Credit Cards	Amount
TOTAL	

TOTAL EXPENSES	
Total Fixed Expenses	
Total Installment Expenses	
Total Monthly Expenses from Below	
GRAND TOTAL	

	RECREATION		EDUCATION			FAMILY			GENERAL						
vacation trips	entertain. video movie music parties	lottery sports hobbies lessons clubs	computer upgrades software supplies service	seminar workshop tuition supplies	newspaper books magazines games	elder care child care sitter tutor	infant exp. allowance school exp. toys arcades	pet vet supplies services		gifts cards flowers	charitable contribut. church temple	work expense dues	prof. services legal CPA investment	other (explanation)
1														
2														
3														
4														
5														
6														
7														
8														
9														
10														
11														
12														
13														
14														
15														
16														
17														
18														
19														
20														
21														
22														
23														
24														
25														
26														
27														
28														
29														
30														
31														
Total														
Budget														
Difference														

MONTHLY EXPENSE RECORD

Balance Forward from Last Month:

Cash _____ Checking _____ Savings _____

NET INCOME				TOTAL
SALARY/COMMISSIONS				
TOTAL INCOME				
OTHER				
TOTAL INCOME				

SAVINGS	
(Describe)	
TOTAL SAVINGS	

INVESTMENTS/RETIREMENT	
TOTAL INVESTMENTS	

	FOOD		HOUSEHOLD						TRANSPORTATION			PERSONAL		HEALTH	
	groceries	fast food / dining out / school / lunches	tobacco / alcohol / snacks / beverages / water	cleaner / mainten. / house / yard / pool	appliances / furniture / furnishings / supplies	postage / ATM fees / bank chg. / misc.	interest / taxes	gas	auto / mainten. / wash / license	taxi / transit / tolls / parking	clothing / alterations / dry clean. / laundry / shoe care	toiletries / cosmetics / hair / nails / massage	doctor / dentist / vision / medicine / vitamins	personal / growth / therapy
WEEK 1 — 1														
2														
3														
4														
5														
6														
7														
WEEK 2 — 8														
9														
10														
11														
12														
13														
14														
WEEK 3 — 15														
16														
17														
18														
19														
20														
21														
WEEK 4 — 22														
23														
24														
25														
26														
27														
28														
29														
30														
31														
Total														
Budget														
Difference														

MONTHLY EXPENSE RECORD

FIXED EXPENSES			
Monthly	Amount	Monthly	Amount
Mortgage/Rent		Insurance:	
Assn. Fee		House/Apt	
Gas/Fuel		Auto	
Electricity		Life	
Water/Refuse		Health	
Garbage/Sewer		Dental	
Telephone		Disability	
Cellular Phone			
Cable/Satellite			
Internet			
Child Support			
Spousal Support			
Health Club			
TOTAL		TOTAL	

INSTALLMENT EXPENSES	
Loans/Credit Cards	Amount
TOTAL	

TOTAL EXPENSES	
Total Fixed Expenses	
Total Installment Expenses	
Total Monthly Expenses from Below	
GRAND TOTAL	

	RECREATION			EDUCATION			FAMILY			GENERAL					
vacation trips	entertain. video movie music parties	lottery sports hobbies lessons clubs	computer upgrades software supplies service	seminar workshop tuition supplies	newspaper books magazines games	elder care child care sitter tutor	infant exp. allowance school exp. toys arcades	pet vet supplies services	gifts cards flowers	charitable contribut. church temple	work expense dues	prof. services legal CPA investment	other (explanation)		
1															
2															
3															
4															
5															
6															
7															
8															
9															
10															
11															
12															
13															
14															
15															
16															
17															
18															
19															
20															
21															
22															
23															
24															
25															
26															
27															
28															
29															
30															
31															
Total															
Budget															
Difference															

MONTHLY EXPENSE RECORD

Balance Forward from Last Month:

Cash _____ Checking _____ Savings _____

NET INCOME			
			TOTAL
SALARY/COMMISSIONS			
		TOTAL INCOME	
OTHER			
		TOTAL INCOME	

SAVINGS	
(Describe)	
TOTAL SAVINGS	

INVESTMENTS/RETIREMENT	
TOTAL INVESTMENTS	

	FOOD		HOUSEHOLD						TRANSPORTATION			PERSONAL		HEALTH	
	groceries	fast food dining out school lunches	tobacco alcohol snacks beverages water	cleaner mainten. house yard pool	appliances furniture furnishings supplies	postage ATM fees bank chg. misc.	interest taxes	gas	auto mainten. wash license	taxi transit tolls parking	clothing alterations dry clean. laundry shoe care	toiletries cosmetics hair nails massage	doctor dentist vision medicine vitamins	personal growth therapy
WEEK 1	1													
	2													
	3													
	4													
	5													
	6													
	7													
WEEK 2	8													
	9													
	10													
	11													
	12													
	13													
	14													
WEEK 3	15													
	16													
	17													
	18													
	19													
	20													
	21													
WEEK 4	22													
	23													
	24													
	25													
	26													
	27													
	28													
	29													
	30													
	31													
	Total													
	Budget													
	Difference													

MONTHLY EXPENSE RECORD

FIXED EXPENSES

Monthly	Amount	Monthly	Amount
Mortgage/Rent		Insurance:	
Assn. Fee		House/Apt	
Gas/Fuel		Auto	
Electricity		Life	
Water/Refuse		Health	
Garbage/Sewer		Dental	
Telephone		Disability	
Cellular Phone			
Cable/Satellite			
Internet			
Child Support			
Spousal Support			
Health Club			
TOTAL		**TOTAL**	

INSTALLMENT EXPENSES

Loans/Credit Cards	Amount
TOTAL	

TOTAL EXPENSES

Total Fixed Expenses	
Total Installment Expenses	
Total Monthly Expenses from Below	
GRAND TOTAL	

	RECREATION		EDUCATION			FAMILY			GENERAL						
vacation trips	entertain. video movie music parties	lottery sports hobbies lessons clubs	computer upgrades software supplies service	seminar workshop tuition supplies	newspaper books magazines games	elder care child care sitter tutor	infant exp. allowance school exp. toys arcades	pet vet supplies services		gifts cards flowers	charitable contribut. church temple	work expense dues	prof. services legal CPA investment	other (explanation)
1															
2															
3															
4															
5															
6															
7															
8															
9															
10															
11															
12															
13															
14															
15															
16															
17															
18															
19															
20															
21															
22															
23															
24															
25															
26															
27															
28															
29															
30															
31															
Total															
Budget															
Difference															

MONTHLY EXPENSE RECORD

Balance Forward from Last Month:

Cash _____ Checking _____ Savings _____

NET INCOME				TOTAL
SALARY/COMMISSIONS				
TOTAL INCOME				
OTHER				
TOTAL INCOME				

SAVINGS	
(Describe)	
TOTAL SAVINGS	

INVESTMENTS/RETIREMENT	
TOTAL INVESTMENTS	

	FOOD		HOUSEHOLD						TRANSPORTATION			PERSONAL		HEALTH	
	groceries	fast food dining out school lunches	tobacco alcohol snacks beverages water	cleaner mainten. house yard pool	appliances furniture furnishings supplies	postage ATM fees bank chg. misc.	interest taxes	gas	auto mainten. wash license	taxi transit tolls parking	clothing alterations dry clean. laundry shoe care	toiletries cosmetics hair nails massage	doctor dentist vision medicine vitamins	personal growth therapy
WEEK 1														
1														
2														
3														
4														
5														
6														
7														
WEEK 2														
8														
9														
10														
11														
12														
13														
14														
WEEK 3														
15														
16														
17														
18														
19														
20														
21														
WEEK 4														
22														
23														
24														
25														
26														
27														
28														
29														
30														
31														
Total														
Budget														
Difference														

MONTHLY EXPENSE RECORD

FIXED EXPENSES

Monthly	Amount	Monthly	Amount
Mortgage/Rent		Insurance:	
Assn. Fee		House/Apt	
Gas/Fuel		Auto	
Electricity		Life	
Water/Refuse		Health	
Garbage/Sewer		Dental	
Telephone		Disability	
Cellular Phone			
Cable/Satellite			
Internet			
Child Support			
Spousal Support			
Health Club			
TOTAL		**TOTAL**	

INSTALLMENT EXPENSES

Loans/Credit Cards	Amount
TOTAL	

TOTAL EXPENSES

Total Fixed Expenses	
Total Installment Expenses	
Total Monthly Expenses from Below	
GRAND TOTAL	

	RECREATION		EDUCATION		FAMILY			GENERAL						
vacation trips	entertain. video movie music parties	lottery sports hobbies lessons clubs	computer upgrades software supplies service	seminar workshop tuition supplies	newspaper books magazines games	elder care child care sitter tutor	infant exp. allowance school exp. toys arcades	pet vet supplies services	gifts cards flowers	charitable contribut. church temple	work expense dues	prof. services legal CPA investment	other (explanation)
1														
2														
3														
4														
5														
6														
7														
8														
9														
10														
11														
12														
13														
14														
15														
16														
17														
18														
19														
20														
21														
22														
23														
24														
25														
26														
27														
28														
29														
30														
31														
Total														
Budget														
Difference														

MONTHLY EXPENSE RECORD

Balance Forward from Last Month:

Cash _____ Checking _____ Savings _____

NET INCOME			TOTAL
SALARY/COMMISSIONS			
TOTAL INCOME			
OTHER			
TOTAL INCOME			

SAVINGS	
(Describe)	
TOTAL SAVINGS	

INVESTMENTS/RETIREMENT	
TOTAL INVESTMENTS	

	FOOD		HOUSEHOLD						TRANSPORTATION			PERSONAL		HEALTH	
	groceries	fast food dining out school lunches	tobacco alcohol snacks beverages water	cleaner mainten. house yard pool	appliances furniture furnishings supplies	postage ATM fees bank chg. misc.	interest taxes	gas	auto mainten. wash license	taxi transit tolls parking	clothing alterations dry clean. laundry shoe care	toiletries cosmetics hair nails massage	doctor dentist vision medicine vitamins	personal growth therapy
WEEK 1	1													
	2													
	3													
	4													
	5													
	6													
	7													
WEEK 2	8													
	9													
	10													
	11													
	12													
	13													
	14													
WEEK 3	15													
	16													
	17													
	18													
	19													
	20													
	21													
WEEK 4	22													
	23													
	24													
	25													
	26													
	27													
	28													
	29													
	30													
	31													
	Total													
	Budget													
	Difference													

MONTHLY EXPENSE RECORD

FIXED EXPENSES

Monthly	Amount	Monthly	Amount
Mortgage/Rent		Insurance:	
Assn. Fee		House/Apt	
Gas/Fuel		Auto	
Electricity		Life	
Water/Refuse		Health	
Garbage/Sewer		Dental	
Telephone		Disability	
Cellular Phone			
Cable/Satellite			
Internet			
Child Support			
Spousal Support			
Health Club			
TOTAL		**TOTAL**	

INSTALLMENT EXPENSES

Loans/Credit Cards	Amount
TOTAL	

TOTAL EXPENSES

Total Fixed Expenses	
Total Installment Expenses	
Total Monthly Expenses from Below	
GRAND TOTAL	

	RECREATION			EDUCATION		FAMILY			GENERAL						
vacation trips	entertain. video movie music parties	lottery sports hobbies lessons clubs	computer upgrades software supplies service	seminar workshop tuition supplies	newspaper books magazines games	elder care child care sitter tutor	infant exp. allowance school exp. toys arcades	pet vet supplies services	gifts cards flowers	charitable contribut. church temple	work expense dues	prof. services legal CPA investment	other (explanation)		
1															
2															
3															
4															
5															
6															
7															
8															
9															
10															
11															
12															
13															
14															
15															
16															
17															
18															
19															
20															
21															
22															
23															
24															
25															
26															
27															
28															
29															
30															
31															
Total															
Budget															
Difference															

MONTHLY EXPENSE RECORD

NET INCOME				TOTAL
SALARY/COMMISSIONS				
TOTAL INCOME				
OTHER				
TOTAL INCOME				

SAVINGS	
(Describe)	
TOTAL SAVINGS	

INVESTMENTS/RETIREMENT	
TOTAL INVESTMENTS	

	FOOD		HOUSEHOLD						TRANSPORTATION			PERSONAL		HEALTH	
	groceries	fast food dining out school lunches	tobacco alcohol snacks beverages water	cleaner mainten. house yard pool	appliances furniture furnishings supplies	postage ATM fees bank chg. misc.	interest taxes	gas	auto mainten. wash license	taxi transit tolls parking	clothing alterations dry clean. laundry shoe care	toiletries cosmetics hair nails massage	doctor dentist vision medicine vitamins	personal growth therapy
W E E K 1	1													
	2													
	3													
	4													
	5													
	6													
	7													
W E E K 2	8													
	9													
	10													
	11													
	12													
	13													
	14													
W E E K 3	15													
	16													
	17													
	18													
	19													
	20													
	21													
W E E K 4	22													
	23													
	24													
	25													
	26													
	27													
	28													
	29													
	30													
	31													
	Total													
	Budget													
	Difference													

MONTHLY EXPENSE RECORD

FIXED EXPENSES

Monthly	Amount	Monthly	Amount
Mortgage/Rent		Insurance:	
Assn. Fee		House/Apt	
Gas/Fuel		Auto	
Electricity		Life	
Water/Refuse		Health	
Garbage/Sewer		Dental	
Telephone		Disability	
Cellular Phone			
Cable/Satellite			
Internet			
Child Support			
Spousal Support			
Health Club			
TOTAL		**TOTAL**	

INSTALLMENT EXPENSES

Loans/Credit Cards	Amount
TOTAL	

TOTAL EXPENSES

Total Fixed Expenses	
Total Installment Expenses	
Total Monthly Expenses from Below	
GRAND TOTAL	

	RECREATION			EDUCATION			FAMILY				GENERAL					
vacation trips	entertain. video movie music parties	lottery sports hobbies lessons clubs	computer upgrades software supplies service	seminar workshop tuition supplies	newspaper books magazines games	elder care child care sitter tutor	infant exp. allowance school exp. toys arcades	pet vet supplies services		gifts cards flowers	charitable contribut. church temple	work expense dues	prof. services legal CPA investment	other (explanation)
1														
2														
3														
4														
5														
6														
7														
8														
9														
10														
11														
12														
13														
14														
15														
16														
17														
18														
19														
20														
21														
22														
23														
24														
25														
26														
27														
28														
29														
30														
31														
Total														
Budget														
Difference														

MONTHLY EXPENSE RECORD

Balance Forward from Last Month:

Cash _____ Checking _____ Savings _____

NET INCOME				TOTAL
SALARY/COMMISSIONS				
TOTAL INCOME				
OTHER				
TOTAL INCOME				

SAVINGS	
(Describe)	
TOTAL SAVINGS	

INVESTMENTS/RETIREMENT	
TOTAL INVESTMENTS	

	FOOD			HOUSEHOLD					TRANSPORTATION		PERSONAL		HEALTH	
	groceries	fast food dining out school lunches	tobacco alcohol snacks beverages water	cleaner mainten. house yard pool	appliances furniture furnishings supplies	postage ATM fees bank chg. misc.	interest taxes	gas	auto mainten. wash license	taxi transit tolls parking	clothing alterations dry clean. laundry shoe care	toiletries cosmetics hair nails massage	doctor dentist vision medicine vitamins	personal growth therapy
WEEK 1	1													
	2													
	3													
	4													
	5													
	6													
	7													
WEEK 2	8													
	9													
	10													
	11													
	12													
	13													
	14													
WEEK 3	15													
	16													
	17													
	18													
	19													
	20													
	21													
WEEK 4	22													
	23													
	24													
	25													
	26													
	27													
	28													
	29													
	30													
	31													
	Total													
	Budget													
	Difference													

MONTHLY EXPENSE RECORD

AUGUST

FIXED EXPENSES

Monthly	Amount	Monthly	Amount
Mortgage/Rent		Insurance:	
Assn. Fee		House/Apt	
Gas/Fuel		Auto	
Electricity		Life	
Water/Refuse		Health	
Garbage/Sewer		Dental	
Telephone		Disability	
Cellular Phone			
Cable/Satellite			
Internet			
Child Support			
Spousal Support			
Health Club			
TOTAL		**TOTAL**	

INSTALLMENT EXPENSES

Loans/Credit Cards	Amount
TOTAL	

TOTAL EXPENSES

Total Fixed Expenses	
Total Installment Expenses	
Total Monthly Expenses from Below	
GRAND TOTAL	

	RECREATION		EDUCATION		FAMILY			GENERAL						
vacation trips	entertain. video movie music parties	lottery sports hobbies lessons clubs	computer upgrades software supplies service	seminar workshop tuition supplies	newspaper books magazines games	elder care child care sitter tutor	infant exp. allowance school exp. toys arcades	pet vet supplies services	gifts cards flowers	charitable contribut. church temple	work expense dues	prof. services legal CPA investment	other (explanation)
1														
2														
3														
4														
5														
6														
7														
8														
9														
10														
11														
12														
13														
14														
15														
16														
17														
18														
19														
20														
21														
22														
23														
24														
25														
26														
27														
28														
29														
30														
31														
Total														
Budget														
Difference														

MONTHLY EXPENSE RECORD

Balance Forward from Last Month:

Cash _____ Checking _____ Savings _____

NET INCOME				
				TOTAL
SALARY/COMMISSIONS				
			TOTAL INCOME	
OTHER				
			TOTAL INCOME	

SAVINGS	
(Describe)	
TOTAL SAVINGS	

INVESTMENTS/RETIREMENT	
TOTAL INVESTMENTS	

	FOOD	HOUSEHOLD							TRANSPORTATION		PERSONAL		HEALTH	
	groceries	fast food dining out school lunches	tobacco alcohol snacks beverages water	cleaner mainten. house yard pool	appliances furniture furnishings supplies	postage ATM fees bank chg. misc.	interest taxes	gas	auto mainten. wash license	taxi transit tolls parking	clothing alterations dry clean. laundry shoe care	toiletries cosmetics hair nails massage	doctor dentist vision medicine vitamins	personal growth therapy
WEEK 1	1													
	2													
	3													
	4													
	5													
	6													
	7													
WEEK 2	8													
	9													
	10													
	11													
	12													
	13													
	14													
WEEK 3	15													
	16													
	17													
	18													
	19													
	20													
	21													
WEEK 4	22													
	23													
	24													
	25													
	26													
	27													
	28													
	29													
	30													
	31													
	Total													
	Budget													
	Difference													

MONTHLY EXPENSE RECORD

FIXED EXPENSES

Monthly	Amount	Monthly	Amount
Mortgage/Rent		Insurance:	
Assn. Fee		House/Apt	
Gas/Fuel		Auto	
Electricity		Life	
Water/Refuse		Health	
Garbage/Sewer		Dental	
Telephone		Disability	
Cellular Phone			
Cable/Satellite			
Internet			
Child Support			
Spousal Support			
Health Club			
TOTAL		**TOTAL**	

INSTALLMENT EXPENSES

Loans/Credit Cards	Amount
TOTAL	

TOTAL EXPENSES

Total Fixed Expenses	
Total Installment Expenses	
Total Monthly Expenses from Below	
GRAND TOTAL	

RECREATION			EDUCATION		FAMILY		GENERAL							
vacation trips	entertain. video movie music parties	lottery sports hobbies lessons clubs	computer upgrades software supplies service	seminar workshop tuition supplies	newspaper books magazines games	elder care child care sitter tutor	infant exp. allowance school exp. toys arcades	pet vet supplies services		gifts cards flowers	charitable contribut. church temple	work expense dues	prof. services legal CPA investment	other (explanation)
1														
2														
3														
4														
5														
6														
7														
8														
9														
10														
11														
12														
13														
14														
15														
16														
17														
18														
19														
20														
21														
22														
23														
24														
25														
26														
27														
28														
29														
30														
31														
Total														
Budget														
Difference														

MONTHLY EXPENSE RECORD

Balance Forward from Last Month:

Cash _____ Checking _____ Savings _____

NET INCOME				TOTAL
SALARY/COMMISSIONS				
TOTAL INCOME				
OTHER				
TOTAL INCOME				

SAVINGS	
(Describe)	
TOTAL SAVINGS	

INVESTMENTS/RETIREMENT	
TOTAL INVESTMENTS	

	FOOD	HOUSEHOLD					TRANSPORTATION			PERSONAL		HEALTH	
	groceries	fast food / dining out / school / lunches	tobacco / alcohol / snacks / beverages / water	cleaner / mainten. / house / yard / pool	appliances / furniture / furnishings / supplies	postage / ATM fees / bank chg. / misc.	interest / taxes	gas	auto / mainten. / wash / license	taxi / transit / tolls / parking	clothing / alterations / dry clean. / laundry / shoe care	toiletries / cosmetics / hair / nails / massage	doctor / dentist / vision / medicine / vitamins	personal / growth / therapy
WEEK 1 — 1														
2														
3														
4														
5														
6														
7														
WEEK 2 — 8														
9														
10														
11														
12														
13														
14														
WEEK 3 — 15														
16														
17														
18														
19														
20														
21														
WEEK 4 — 22														
23														
24														
25														
26														
27														
28														
29														
30														
31														
Total														
Budget														
Difference														

MONTHLY EXPENSE RECORD

FIXED EXPENSES

Monthly	Amount	Monthly	Amount
Mortgage/Rent		Insurance:	
Assn. Fee		House/Apt	
Gas/Fuel		Auto	
Electricity		Life	
Water/Refuse		Health	
Garbage/Sewer		Dental	
Telephone		Disability	
Cellular Phone			
Cable/Satellite			
Internet			
Child Support			
Spousal Support			
Health Club			
TOTAL		**TOTAL**	

INSTALLMENT EXPENSES

Loans/Credit Cards	Amount
TOTAL	

TOTAL EXPENSES

Total Fixed Expenses	
Total Installment Expenses	
Total Monthly Expenses from Below	
GRAND TOTAL	

	RECREATION		EDUCATION		FAMILY		GENERAL						
vacation trips	entertain. video movie music parties	lottery sports hobbies lessons clubs	computer upgrades software supplies service	seminar workshop tuition supplies	newspaper books magazines games	elder care child care sitter tutor	infant exp. allowance school exp. toys arcades	pet vet supplies services	gifts cards flowers	charitable contribut. church temple	work expense dues	prof. services legal CPA investment	other (explanation)
1													
2													
3													
4													
5													
6													
7													
8													
9													
10													
11													
12													
13													
14													
15													
16													
17													
18													
19													
20													
21													
22													
23													
24													
25													
26													
27													
28													
29													
30													
31													
Total													
Budget													
Difference													

MONTHLY EXPENSE RECORD

Balance Forward from Last Month:

Cash _____ Checking _____ Savings _____

NET INCOME				
				TOTAL
SALARY/COMMISSIONS				
			TOTAL INCOME	
OTHER				
			TOTAL INCOME	

SAVINGS	
(Describe)	
TOTAL SAVINGS	

INVESTMENTS/RETIREMENT	
TOTAL INVESTMENTS	

	FOOD		HOUSEHOLD						TRANSPORTATION		PERSONAL		HEALTH	
	groceries	fast food / dining out / school / lunches	tobacco / alcohol / snacks / beverages / water	cleaner / mainten. / house / yard / pool	appliances / furniture / furnishings / supplies	postage / ATM fees / bank chg. / misc.	interest / taxes	gas	auto / mainten. / wash / license	taxi / transit / tolls / parking	clothing / alterations / dry clean. / laundry / shoe care	toiletries / cosmetics / hair / nails / massage	doctor / dentist / vision / medicine / vitamins	personal / growth / therapy
W E E K 1	1													
	2													
	3													
	4													
	5													
	6													
	7													
W E E K 2	8													
	9													
	10													
	11													
	12													
	13													
	14													
W E E K 3	15													
	16													
	17													
	18													
	19													
	20													
	21													
W E E K 4	22													
	23													
	24													
	25													
	26													
	27													
	28													
	29													
	30													
	31													
	Total													
	Budget													
	Difference													

MONTHLY EXPENSE RECORD

FIXED EXPENSES

Monthly	Amount	Monthly	Amount
Mortgage/Rent		Insurance:	
Assn. Fee		House/Apt	
Gas/Fuel		Auto	
Electricity		Life	
Water/Refuse		Health	
Garbage/Sewer		Dental	
Telephone		Disability	
Cellular Phone			
Cable/Satellite			
Internet			
Child Support			
Spousal Support			
Health Club			
TOTAL		**TOTAL**	

INSTALLMENT EXPENSES

Loans/Credit Cards	Amount
TOTAL	

TOTAL EXPENSES

Total Fixed Expenses	
Total Installment Expenses	
Total Monthly Expenses from Below	
GRAND TOTAL	

	RECREATION		EDUCATION		FAMILY			GENERAL						
vacation trips	entertain. video movie music parties	lottery sports hobbies lessons clubs	computer upgrades software supplies service	seminar workshop tuition supplies	newspaper books magazines games	elder care child care sitter tutor	infant exp. allowance school exp. toys arcades	pet vet supplies services		gifts cards flowers	charitable contribut. church temple	work expense dues	prof. services legal CPA investment	other (explanation)
1														
2														
3														
4														
5														
6														
7														
8														
9														
10														
11														
12														
13														
14														
15														
16														
17														
18														
19														
20														
21														
22														
23														
24														
25														
26														
27														
28														
29														
30														
31														
Total														
Budget														
Difference														

MONTHLY EXPENSE RECORD

Balance Forward from Last Month:

Cash _____ Checking _____ Savings _____

NET INCOME

				TOTAL
SALARY/COMMISSIONS				
TOTAL INCOME				
OTHER				
TOTAL INCOME				

SAVINGS

(Describe)	
TOTAL SAVINGS	

INVESTMENTS/RETIREMENT

TOTAL INVESTMENTS	

	FOOD		HOUSEHOLD						TRANSPORTATION			PERSONAL		HEALTH	
	groceries	fast food dining out school lunches	tobacco alcohol snacks beverages water	cleaner mainten. house yard pool	appliances furniture furnishings supplies	postage ATM fees bank chg. misc.	interest taxes	gas	auto mainten. wash license	taxi transit tolls parking	clothing alterations dry clean. laundry shoe care	toiletries cosmetics hair nails massage	doctor dentist vision medicine vitamins	personal growth therapy
WEEK 1	1													
	2													
	3													
	4													
	5													
	6													
	7													
WEEK 2	8													
	9													
	10													
	11													
	12													
	13													
	14													
WEEK 3	15													
	16													
	17													
	18													
	19													
	20													
	21													
WEEK 4	22													
	23													
	24													
	25													
	26													
	27													
	28													
	29													
	30													
	31													
	Total													
	Budget													
	Difference													

MONTHLY EXPENSE RECORD

FIXED EXPENSES

Monthly	Amount	Monthly	Amount
Mortgage/Rent		Insurance:	
Assn. Fee		House/Apt	
Gas/Fuel		Auto	
Electricity		Life	
Water/Refuse		Health	
Garbage/Sewer		Dental	
Telephone		Disability	
Cellular Phone			
Cable/Satellite			
Internet			
Child Support			
Spousal Support			
Health Club			
TOTAL		**TOTAL**	

INSTALLMENT EXPENSES

Loans/Credit Cards	Amount
TOTAL	

TOTAL EXPENSES

Total Fixed Expenses	
Total Installment Expenses	
Total Monthly Expenses from Below	
GRAND TOTAL	

	RECREATION			EDUCATION			FAMILY		GENERAL						
vacation trips	entertain. video movie music parties	lottery sports hobbies lessons clubs	computer upgrades software supplies service	seminar workshop tuition supplies	newspaper books magazines games	elder care child care sitter tutor	infant exp. allowance school exp. toys arcades	pet vet supplies services		gifts cards flowers	charitable contribut. church temple	work expense dues	prof. services legal CPA investment	other (explanation)
1															
2															
3															
4															
5															
6															
7															
8															
9															
10															
11															
12															
13															
14															
15															
16															
17															
18															
19															
20															
21															
22															
23															
24															
25															
26															
27															
28															
29															
30															
31															
Total															
Budget															
Difference															

Summary-for-the-Year Record/End-of-the-Year Tax Information

The totals you have at the end of each month on the **Monthly Expense Record** can be transferred to this section so you will have a total picture and a way to compare monthly expenses for each category. This **Summary-for-the-Year Record** is excellent for meas-uring your financial progress and setting your future goals. **The End-of-the-Year Tax Information** worksheet offers a place to record your pay stub deduction information, such as your taxes, FICA, 401(k), 403(b), and other deductions.

SUMMARY-FOR-THE-YEAR RECORD

		JAN.	FEB.	MAR.	APR.	MAY	JUNE	JULY	AUG.	SEPT.	OCT.	NOV.	DEC.	Total	Mo. Avg.
Net Income	Salary/Commission														
	Other														
Food	Groceries														
	School Lunches, Dine Out, Fast Food														
	Snacks, Beverages, Alcohol, Tobacco														
Household	Supplies, Cleaners, Maintenance, House, Yard, Pool														
	Appliances, Furniture, Furnishings, Supplies														
	Postage, ATM Fees, Bank Charges, Misc.														
	Interest, Taxes														
Transportation	Gas														
	Automobile Maintenance, Wash, License														
	Transit, Tolls, Taxi, Parking														
Personal	Clothing, Alterations, Dry Cleaning, Laundry, Shoe Care														
	Cosmetics, Hair, Nails, Massage, Toiletries														
Health	Doctor, Dentist, Vision, Medicine, Vitamins														
	Personal Growth Therapy														
Recreation	Vacation, Trips														
	Entertain., DVD, Movies, Music, Parties														
	Sports, Hobbies, Lessons, Clubs, Lottery														
	Computer, Upgrades, Software, Supplies, Service														

SUMMARY FOR MONTHLY SAVINGS/INVESTMENTS/RETIREMENT

	JAN.	FEB.	MAR.	APR.	MAY	JUNE	JULY	AUG.	SEPT.	OCT.	NOV.	DEC.	Total
Savings													
Investments													
Retirement													
Total													

		JAN.	FEB.	MAR.	APR.	MAY	JUNE	JULY	AUG.	SEPT.	OCT.	NOV.	DEC.	**Total**	**Mo. Avg.**
Education	Tuition, Supplies, Workshops, Seminars														
	Books, Magazines, Software, Newspaper, Games														
Family	Elder Care, Child Care, Sitter, Tutor														
	Allowance, Toys, Infant Exp., School Exp., Arcades														
	Pet, Vet, Supplies, Services														
General	Gifts, Cards, Flowers														
	Charitable Contribut., Church, Temple														
	Work Expense, Dues														
	Prof. Serv., Legal, CPA, Investment														
	Other														
Home	Mortgage, Rent, Assn. Fees														
Utilities	Gas, Electric														
	Water, Garbage														
	Phone, Cable, ISP														
Support	Child, Spousal, Club														
Insurance	Home, Auto, Life, Health, Disability														
Installment	Loans, Credit Cards														
Total	Monthly Expenses														

END-OF-THE-YEAR TAX INFORMATION

	JAN.	FEB.	MAR.	APR.	MAY	JUNE	JULY	AUG.	SEPT.	OCT.	NOV.	DEC.	**Total**
Federal													
State													
FICA													
Other Deductions													
Total													

This collection of worksheets for keeping records and recording expenses will help you keep your financial records organized. Look through each of these forms to see which worksheets apply to you and will be helpful for your particular household's financial situation.

- **Medical Expense Record**

- **Flexible Spending Account Record**

- **Tax-Deductible Expense Record**

- **Miscellaneous Expense Record**

- **Investment/Savings Record**

- **Child Support Records**

- **Subscription Record**

- **Online and Mail Order Purchase Record**

Medical Expense Record

If you need to keep additional records on medical expenses, use these worksheets. The first page, Doctor, Dentist, and Hospital Visits, can be used for recording all visits including nontraditional health care. Include the costs here whether they are full pay, co-pay, or are going to be reimbursed by insurance. If you have a lot of prescriptions, lab tests, and other related medical expenses (like glasses, crutches, rental medical equipment), then use the second page, Medical Expenses, Prescriptions, and Other to keep those expense records separate.

Again, these worksheets are a guideline so adjust them to work for your medical recordkeeping needs.

A space is provided for mileage, which at this writing is tax-deductible. The columns for "Date Submitted" and "Insurance Reimbursements" are provided for those households paying the medical bills first before submitting claims or paying the differences not covered by insurance and wanting to keep this information separate.

During tax time this information will save you hours of preparation time.

MEDICAL EXPENSE RECORD

DOCTOR, DENTIST, AND HOSPITAL VISITS					
Date	Mileage	To Whom Paid	Amount	Date Submitted	Insurance Reimbursements Amount/Date Paid
		Total			
		Total Amount Paid			
		Total Reimbursed			
		Total Medical Cost			

MEDICAL EXPENSE RECORD

MEDICAL EXPENSES, PRESCRIPTIONS, AND OTHER					
Date	Mileage	To Whom Paid	Amount	Date Submitted	Insurance Reimbursements Amount/Date Paid
Total					
Total Amount Paid					
Total Reimbursed					
Total Medical Cost					

Flexible Spending Account Record

More companies are offering flexible spending accounts (FSAs), which allow their employees to save pretax dollars for certain health care and dependent day care expenses. Your employer will explain how the program works, the maximum contribution amounts, and qualifying expenses, and will give you estimating worksheets so you can determine how much money to plan to contribute to your FSA.

These accounts can be very valuable if you use them to their fullest advantage and diligently keep your records and receipts. The tricky part is carefully balancing what you believe will be all the estimated expenses against the actual total expenses at the end of the year. Because this is a "use it or lose it" program, you face the risk of forfeiting any unused money at the end of the year. Therefore, the purpose of this **Flexible Spending Account Record** is to provide a form for all your records so that you don't miss any qualifying expenses. Be sure to have a folder where you keep all the matching receipts. All of this information will be required at the end of the year.

FLEXIBLE SPENDING ACCOUNT RECORD

Each account must be separate. Money in one account cannot be used for the other account.

Health Care Expenses (Medical, Dental, Vision Deductibles, Copays, Coinsurance, Prescription Copays, Other)
Dependent Care Expenses (Child/Elder Care, Eligible School & Summer Programs, Kindergarten/Nursery School Expenses)

Date	Description of Expense	Cost	Date Claim Submitted	Reimbursed	Notes

Tax-Deductible Expense Record

After you record your expenses on the **Monthly Expense Record** worksheets, take a moment to jot down deductible expenses on the **Tax-Deductible Expense Record** so you have all your deductible expenses recorded in one place. When you prepare next year's tax return, itemizing deductions will be a very quick and efficient process.

Each year, tax deductions may vary. This worksheet is designed to be a convenient record of all deductions applying to your circumstances and the current tax laws. Include categories such as education, professional or union dues, child care, alimony, casualty losses, etc. If you have regular or multiple deductions in one category, the **Multiple Tax-Deductible Expense Record** may be more convenient for recording those amounts.

Consult your tax professional regarding any changes in tax law for these or any other tax-related records.

"The IRS audited my records and said they were so good it was no problem and they accepted all of it. My insurance company also accepted my records without having receipts. I'm 68 years old and have used this book for ten years and I'm buying ten more for the next ten years."

More and more households seem to be starting up small home businesses or getting into different kinds of network marketing to generate extra income. The next step is a basic system for recording business income and expenses to be better prepared for taxes. *The Budget Kit* does offer the same basic concepts that one would use for personal budgeting as well as budgeting for a small business; however, I prefer to recommend some dedicated business resources.

The following two resources are simple and straightforward, giving you all the basic tools you need for organizing your home business and tax records:

Tax Minimi$er™ — For Small and Home-Based Businesses and Self-Employed Entrepreneurs, The Daily Plan-It, LLC, *www.taxminimiser.com*

It's How Much You Keep That Counts! Not How Much You Make. The ONLY 'Plain English' Step-by-Step Guide to Home-Business Tax Breaks Authorized by Congress, Ronald R. Mueller, MBA, Ph.D., *www.HomeBusinessTaxSavings.com*

TAX-DEDUCTIBLE EXPENSE RECORD

Date	Description (Donation/Payment To)	Check Number	Amount/Value: Taxes/ Interest	Charitable Contribution	_____	_____
	Total					

MULTIPLE TAX-DEDUCTIBLE EXPENSE RECORD

CATEGORY: _____

Date	Description	Amount
		Total

CATEGORY: _____

Date	Description	Amount
		Total

Miscellaneous Expense Record

A variety of additional generic worksheets are provided for other records, such as major household purchases, home improvement projects, car expenses, and college costs. Use any of these or the other variety of worksheets in this workbook to best fit your particular needs.

RECORD OF _____   **MISCELLANEOUS EXPENSE RECORD YEAR 20___**

	JAN.	FEB.	MAR.	APR.	MAY	JUNE	JULY	AUG.	SEPT.	OCT.	NOV.	DEC.	TOTAL
Total													

MISCELLANEOUS EXPENSE RECORD

Date	To Whom Paid/Service	Amount
	Total	

Date	To Whom Paid/Service	Amount
	Total	

Investment/Savings Record

Your Investment Picture

If you followed the suggestions and guidelines in this workbook, you probably already have or soon will have some basic savings and investments.

Whether you have money in company savings plans, inherited some stocks and bonds, invested in mutual funds, changed your savings from pass-books to certificates of deposit (CDs) or money markets, or opened a Roth or traditional individual retirement account (IRA), it is important to keep all your records in one place and know what you have. These records are extremely useful for preparing income tax, completing financial statements, and helping your heirs in the event of an unexpected death.

As with personal finances, if you don't pay attention to your investments or keep careful records of them, you may easily forget what you have or where you have them. Soon it may be hard to remember just exactly where you put those IRAs that you purchased sometime in 1996 or 2001. What rates are they getting? What are the maturity dates?

Or maybe through your parents or a divorce, you acquired some stocks that are just "sitting" in an account and you really don't know what you have. With today's fast-paced lifestyle, it is easy to leave the responsibility of knowing what you own to someone else—a banker, a broker, or an accountant—but by doing so, you sacrifice an understanding and awareness of your total financial picture.

The **Investment/Savings Record** provides a place for recording key information about your various investments. The space on the right allows for a periodic follow-up of your current yield. The headings are used as a guideline. If necessary, change them to make them appropriate for your investments.

If you anticipate frequent changes, you should record general information at the beginning of the year here and use the other worksheets in this section of the workbook to record your investment and savings activity. You can modify the **Savings Activity Record, Retirement Savings Record,** or **Miscellaneous Expense Record** to fit your needs. The important point is to be sure that you have recorded all the information for each of your investments and have it all in one convenient place.

Reserve Funds

Use this section of the **Investment/Savings Record** to record information about your liquid-asset accounts (money you have available for immediate use without withdrawal penalties). These include investments in money market accounts or savings in your bank and/or credit union.

If you have ongoing monthly savings activity, you can use the **Savings Activity Record** to record your month-to-month transactions. On that page, you can list your savings for upcoming taxes or insurance (reserve account), unexpected car or home repairs (emergency account), or vacation and Christmas/holiday savings (goal account).

Retirement

Record the information for your retirement savings programs here. Your monthly savings activity can be recorded on the **Retirement Savings Record** in this section. These programs range from savings funded and/or established by your employer, to personal IRAs, Keoghs, tax-sheltered annuities (TSAs), company pensions, and other tax-sheltered investments.

A wide variety of employee-retirement programs are offered through schools, hospitals, government, and private firms. It is easy to forget or ignore these funds for they often are only shown as paycheck deductions. Pay attention to and gather up the necessary information as outlined in this section so you are familiar with your current and past retirement programs.

Short- and Long-Term Holdings

Record your investments held for short or extended periods on the **Investment/Savings Record**. Some of these investments, such as CDs, T-bills, bonds, etc., will have fixed rates or time periods and this information should be noted on the worksheet. With other securities (stocks, mutual funds, and options) prices can change daily. Because there is limited space for all the variable information, use this worksheet for beginning and end-of-the-year summaries.

If you frequently buy and sell, and actively get involved with your investments, you already may have an investment portfolio with all the necessary information. On the other hand, if you do not do much with your investments, especially securities, *the information on this worksheet will be extremely helpful for tax, loan, or net worth purposes.*

Other Investments

Your investments, such as real estate (other than personal residence), collectibles, trusts, or limited or general partnerships, also would be recorded here. If the majority of those other investments are quite extensive, however, you probably have them recorded through another system. If so, indicate where you have those records. The same is true for any of your other investments listed on this worksheet. Be sure your spouse and/or family know where to locate all this information.

Maintaining Control of Your Finances

As you gather your investment information, you may find you need to develop your own follow-up system for those long-range investments with maturity dates. Start a file and keep a copy of these worksheets for each year. Highlight the maturity dates so you have a quick reference.

While reviewing your investments, take time to monitor the returns and determine how well your investments are performing.

These worksheets, along with the others you have used in this workbook, will help you to record all your financial information in one place, thus staying organized and aware of your finances.

THE ONLINE/ELECTRONIC CONNECTION TO *THE BUDGET KIT*

Online banking and investing now available through your bank, brokerage firm, or other services make it possible to keep detailed records of all your savings and investments securely online. Take advantage of the Internet with all the comprehensive financial websites for doing your research and monitoring your investments.

The **Investment/Savings Record** can be used as your basic paper backup information center for your spouse or family when they need to locate your investment information. Keep a summary list of the investments and the URL addresses for the websites you are using. Be sure to include any other contact information, user name, or password that would also be helpful.

INVESTMENT/SAVINGS RECORD

RESERVE FUNDS (Checking, Savings, Money Market, etc.)

Name of Institution	Type	Account Number	Date Opened	Amt. Invested	Interest Rate	Owned By (husband, wife, joint)

RETIREMENT ACCOUNTS (IRA, Roth, 401(k), 403(b), SEP, Keogh, etc.)

Where Held	Type and Name	Account Number	Purchase Date	Amount Invested	Allocation

SHORT- AND LONG-TERM HOLDINGS (Mutual Funds, Stocks, Bonds, etc.)

Where Held	Type and Name	Certificate/ Account Number	Purchase Date	Amount Invested	Number of Shares	Unit Price	Dividend/ Interest Rate

OTHER (Real Estate, Collectibles, etc.)

Location/Name	Date Purchased	Cost	Monthly/Yearly Income	Location of Records

INVESTMENT/SAVINGS RECORD

RESERVE FUNDS

Contact Name/Telephone	Location of Records	Follow-Up Information (date, balance, current yield)

RETIREMENT ACCOUNTS

Owned By (husband, wife, joint)	Contact Name/Telephone	Location of Records	Date Sold	Distribution Amount	Additional Notes (rollover information)

SHORT- AND LONG-TERM HOLDINGS

Date/Amount Dividend Paid	Maturity Date	Owned By (husband, wife, joint)	Contact Name/Telephone	Location of Records	Date Sold	Number of Shares Sold	Net Proceeds	Gain/ Loss

OTHER

Owned By (husband, wife, joint)	Date Sold	Proceeds	Gain/Loss	Additional Notes

SAVINGS ACTIVITY RECORD

EMERGENCY

Institution: _____

Account Number: _____

	JAN.	FEB.	MAR.	APR.	MAY	JUNE	JULY	AUG.	SEPT.	OCT.	NOV.	DEC.
Deposits												
Withdrawals												
Interest Earned												
Balance												

RESERVE

Institution: _____

Account Number: _____

	JAN.	FEB.	MAR.	APR.	MAY	JUNE	JULY	AUG.	SEPT.	OCT.	NOV.	DEC.
Deposits												
Withdrawals												
Interest Earned												
Balance												

GOALS/CHRISTMAS AND HOLIDAY

Institution: _____

Account Number: _____

	JAN.	FEB.	MAR.	APR.	MAY	JUNE	JULY	AUG.	SEPT.	OCT.	NOV.	DEC.
Deposits												
Withdrawals												
Interest Earned												
Balance												

OTHER

Institution: _____

Account Number: _____

	JAN.	FEB.	MAR.	APR.	MAY	JUNE	JULY	AUG.	SEPT.	OCT.	NOV.	DEC.
Deposits												
Withdrawals												
Interest Earned												
Balance												

RETIREMENT SAVINGS RECORD

NAME							

Date	Program (IRA, 401(k), etc.): _____ _____ _____			Program (IRA, 401(k) etc.): Date _____ _____ _____			
Total				**Total**			

NAME							

Date	Program (IRA, 401(k), etc.): _____ _____ _____			Program (IRA, 401(k) etc.): Date _____ _____ _____			
Total				**Total**			

Child Support Records

"Earlier this year I needed a personal loan. I couldn't have qualified if I had no proof of child support. The record in this workbook was sufficient information for the bank's approval."

Keeping Records

After a divorce, it is so easy for depression, anger, fear, and loneliness to interfere with practical thoughts and actions.

During this time, credit problems often crop up. This is not because you are incapable of managing your money, but often because you suddenly are overwhelmed with handling all the aspects of family life and household maintenance. Due dates, bills, and paperwork may just seem to get away from you.

Keeping proper records of child support payments, children's expenses, and pertinent custody information is extremely important. However, because of the demands of trying to meet the physical and emotional needs of your children and yourself, these records often are neglected or are never established.

The following worksheets were designed to help remove some of the burden of keeping important records. The worksheets provide guidelines to help you remember what records you should keep and provide you with a tool for having all your necessary information and records in one place. By organizing and controlling this aspect of your life, you will be better equipped to move on to other pressing issues that you face every day.

If you are the noncustodial parent making the child support payments, recording the information called for can be just as important for you. If you must prove what amount and when a support payment actually was made, received, and cashed, or must prove other significant information for tax or legal purposes, you will have the necessary records.

Utilize and modify the worksheets in this book so that you can record information that is unique to your needs. For example, you may want to use the Medical and Dental Expense section of this workbook for keeping detailed records of who paid a medical expense, the insurance deductible, or the difference not paid by insurance.

When using these worksheets, be aware that the state and federal laws and regulations vary. *The worksheets and text are not a substitute for legal advice from your local attorney. Consult with your attorney for any questions in this section.*

Child Support Payment Record

This record is critical when you need help from your local enforcement agency because of late, short, or missing payments. The "Amount Due" ① column is for the monthly child support payment as ordered. Enter the amount received under the month it was *due*. If no payment was received that month, note that under "Amount Received." ② Because these payments may vary from once a week, or once a month, to sporadically for the year, you will have to modify this column to fit your needs.

Record the other related child support obligations as ordered by the divorce decree, such as medical insurance premium, unreimbursed medical expense, tuition, dues, etc. ③ Also keep records of conversations concerning finances with your case workers, ex-spouse, and others. Keep a copy of your decree, stating the terms, payment, custody, visitation, conditions of support, and your record of conversations in a convenient file.

Note under "Additional Information" ④ if an item was substituted in lieu of a child support payment. Be sure to check with your attorney if this is an *acceptable form of child support*. If you do not wish to accept an item in lieu of a payment, ask your attorney if written notice should be given. If so, be sure to keep a copy.

When recording the institution, number, and date of the check or money order, ⑤ use the symbols shown to indicate how the payment was made. If possible, keep a copy of all checks, money orders, and envelopes, especially if there is a regular problem with support being on time. These copies will be helpful if a court or social agency ever needs to review your records in the event that there is an excessive lag between the date of the check and the date it was sent, or payment was stopped on a check or money order you received. Be sure to note if you are unable to make a copy of the checks, money orders, or envelopes.

You will find that this worksheet will contain some of your most important records. Stay with it.

The Cost of Raising Children

If you need or want to analyze the cost of raising your children, to show the use of support provided, or to demonstrate the need for increased support, use the **Monthly Expense Record** section.

Enter all your children's daily expenses along with all your other expenses on the Monthly Expense Record pages. Modify the headings to fit your individual needs. Use a highlighter, colored pencil, or check mark to show which expenses are the children's. Total the children's expenses in the columns that apply and record the total at the bottom of the page below the family total. If you have a question about allocating expenses shared by you and your children, ask your local attorney.

Another method used by some families for keeping accurate records is a separate checking account and/or a credit card used strictly for children's expenses. Use the method that works best for you.

If you save all your receipts in envelopes labeled for the different categories, you can file these in your filing system.

Child Support Enforcement and Child Visitation Records

In 1984, Congress passed the Child Support Enforcement Amendments of 1984 that strengthen the child support enforcement laws throughout the country. The information you record will be invaluable if you ever need the services of a Child Support Enforcement Bureau in your state to help you collect past-due child support.

If you would like more information about Child Support Enforcement, there is a publication called "Handbook on Child Support Enforcement" available online at *www.acf.hhs.gov/programs/cse/pubs/2005/handbook_on_cse.pdf*. The U.S. Department of Health and Human Services features The Office of Child Support Enforcement website *www.acf.hhs.gov/programs/cse* where you'll find a wealth of additional information.

You can also order the free publication by phone or mail, but you will need to add a $2 service charge. To contact the Federal Citizen Information Center (FCIC), call 888-878-3256 and ask for publication number "505P." Or write to FCIC-07B, P.O. Box 100, Pueblo, CO 81002. Make the check to "Superintendent of Documents." This agency also has a website at *www.pueblo.gsa.gov*. Click on the "Family" section for more publications. While on the website, take a look at their "Money" section for some great publications.

On page 177, there is a basic **Child Visitation Record** form provided to give you a way to record the specific dates of visitation each month. There definitely will be times when this information will be requested, and this can serve as your running documentation.

Reduced Anxiety

These worksheets cannot take away the pain. They can, however, help reduce some of the anxiety associated with the aftermath of a divorce. As you start taking charge of your situation and gain new knowledge, you will regain self-confidence and self-esteem in the process.

Best of luck to you!

CHILD SUPPORT PAYMENT RECORD

Balance Due (from previous year) $ _____

Month	① Amount Due	② Amount Received	⑤ Amount Past Due	Number on: x–$ Order ✓–Check $–Cash	Date on: x–$ Order ✓–Check $–Cash	⑤ Date Payment Received	Institution and Account Number	③ Other Expenses*	④ Additional Information/ Action Taken (check status, gifts, etc.)
JAN.									
FEB.									
MAR.									
APR.									
MAY									
JUNE									
JULY									
AUG.									
SEPT.									
OCT.									
NOV.									
DEC.									
Total									

*Stipulated by decree

CHILD SUPPORT ENFORCEMENT RECORD

Noncustodial Parent

Full Name
_____

Last Known Address(es)
_____
_____
_____

Address Dates _____
Home Telephone
_____

Social Security Number
_____

Birth Date/Place _____
_____

Height _____ Weight _____

Occupation
_____

Last Known Employer(s)
_____
_____

Address
_____
_____
_____

Address Dates _____
Work Telephone
_____

Child Support Enforcement Office

Address
_____
_____
_____

Telephone Number
_____

Case Worker's Name/Telephone
_____
_____

Case Number
_____

Court Order Number
_____

Note: Get a Birth Registration Card from your Vital Statistics Office. This will have all your children's information printed on it so you will have the information handy.

CHILD VISITATION RECORD

DATES OF VISITATION											
JAN.	FEB.	MAR.	APR.	MAY	JUNE	JULY	AUG.	SEPT.	OCT.	NOV.	DEC.

Subscription Record

If you ever waited three months to receive your subscription or learned that your magazine gift took that long before it was ever received, you will appreciate having all this information at your fingertips.

Having this record is an easy way to organize all your subscription amounts and dates due in one central place. It also will help prevent any double payments. You can then transfer this information to the **Yearly Budget Worksheet** in Part Two where all your nonmonthly expenses are listed on one convenient page.

SUBSCRIPTION RECORD

Publication:						
Subscription Through: Agency Address						
Telephone						
Date Ordered						
Amount Paid						
Check# or Credit Card Used						
Length (1, 2, 3 yrs.)						
Expiration Date						
Arrival Date						
Gift For:						
Other						

Online and Mail Order Purchase Record

Mail Order, Internet, and TV Shopping

There are obvious advantages to shopping by mail or online, including convenience, saving time, and discount savings. However, how many times have you ordered something by mail, telephone, or Internet expecting it to arrive, and it never did? Or how about TV infomercials and shopping channels hawking the latest beauty, weight loss, or entertainment products offered with a 30-day money back guarantee? Chances are you have had your share of mail order frustrations, undelivered orders, or unsatisfactory products. You also may have had more items than you care to admit continue to show up each month and be charged to your credit card, because you failed to call and cancel the program after the original product arrived. If so, now you probably recognize the value of keeping clearer records for follow-up and cancellation purposes.

How to Keep Records

If orders do not arrive as scheduled and follow-up action is necessary, this **Online and Mail Order Purchase Record** will be a valuable time and money saver for you.

Use this form for all items ordered even if they are free. Keeping track of rebates also will work on this form. Log the necessary information related to any purchases made by mail, telephone, or online. When you happen to remember an item you ordered some time ago and realize it still has not arrived, you can check these records, see when you ordered the item, then follow up by the appropriate method.

In some cases, it may be easier to cut out the ad with all the information given and tape it to this page or in the back of this workbook. Then fill in only the "Total Sent" and "How Paid" sections. If you order a list of items from one catalog, make a copy of the order form and save it. On this page, make a note of the order, the catalog date, and how and when you paid for it. The same is true for online orders. Print out a copy of the order, including the confirmation number, and save that copy with your records or in the back of this workbook.

When placing a telephone order or following up on an order, be especially careful to record all the information on this worksheet, including the name of the person you spoke to or who took your order.

Safety Online

Shop with the companies you know. If you want to learn more about an unfamiliar company before ordering, ask them to send you information or a catalog. Be sure to find out the company's policies on refunds and returns before placing any order.

Find out if your browser is secure before purchasing anything online. Note if there is a lock icon on the screen. Some browsers use a closed lock icon to indicate a secure session. A secured session is extremely important when you provide personal information such as credit card number, name, address, and phone number over the Internet.

Remember, if you pay with a credit card and have problems with your order, you have the advantage of having the right to dispute your charges. Your creditor will investigate the circumstances while you temporarily withhold payment. The complaint and situation will need to be explained and submitted in writing. Having the records on this page will make that process easier for you.

Be careful with your password. Never give it to anyone. Use a password you can readily remember, but is not as obvious as your birthday, telephone number, license, or Social Security number.

Enjoy these conveniences that now exist, but do so with appropriate caution.

Federal Trade Commission (FTC) Mail Order Rule

The Federal Trade Commission's (FTC) Mail or Telephone Order Merchandising Rule requires companies to ship an order within the time period mentioned in their advertisements. If no time period is given, the company is required to ship an order within 30 days of receipt of your payment. The company must notify you if it cannot make the shipment within 30 days and send you an option notice of either consenting to a delay or canceling the order for a refund.

For more information on e-commerce and the Internet, or consumer information in general, visit *www.ftc.gov/bcp/consumer.shtm*. You will find a wealth of valuable consumer information.

ONLINE AND MAIL ORDER PURCHASE RECORD

Date Ordered					

Item(s) Ordered
   Title
   Description
   Number
   Quantity
   Color					

Source (Internet, magazine, TV, catalog)					
Confirmation Number					

Company Name
   Telephone Number
   Address
   Account No.					

Price					
Total Sent					
How Paid*					
Date Received					
30-Day Return Date					
Cancellation Phone Number					
Follow-Up Notes (date called/wrote, contact person, action taken)					

* credit card, check number, money order, COD, online bill pay

Date Ordered					

Item(s) Ordered
   Title
   Description
   Number
   Quantity
   Color					

Source (Internet, magazine, TV, catalog)					
Confirmation Number					

Company Name
   Telephone Number
   Address
   Account No.					

Price					
Total Sent					
How Paid*					
Date Received					
30-Day Return Date					
Cancellation Phone Number					
Follow-Up Notes (date called/wrote, contact person, action taken)					

* credit card, check number, money order, COD, online bill pay

ONLINE AND MAIL ORDER PURCHASE RECORD

Date Ordered					

Item(s) Ordered
  Title
  Description
  Number
  Quantity
  Color					

Source (Internet, magazine, TV, catalog)					
Confirmation Number					

Company Name
  Telephone Number
  Address
  Account No.					

Price					
Total Sent					
How Paid*					
Date Received					
30-Day Return Date					
Cancellation Phone Number					
Follow-Up Notes (date called/wrote, contact person, action taken)					

* credit card, check number, money order, COD, online bill pay

Date Ordered					

Item(s) Ordered
  Title
  Description
  Number
  Quantity
  Color					

Source (Internet, magazine, TV, catalog)					
Confirmation Number					

Company Name
  Telephone Number
  Address
  Account No.					

Price					
Total Sent					
How Paid*					
Date Received					
30-Day Return Date					
Cancellation Phone Number					
Follow-Up Notes (date called/wrote, contact person, action taken)					

* credit card, check number, money order, COD, online bill pay

Acknowledgments

My special thanks go to the following people who helped with the development of this new and revised version of *The Budget Kit: The Common Cent$ Money Management Workbook*, or gave their support and encouragement during the earlier times as this book metamorphosed through its *Common Cent$* years into the workbook you now hold:

- Shannon Berning, Acquisitions Editor, who encouraged and supported this revision and the talented members of the Kaplan team—Cynthia Ierardo, Development Editor, and Fred Urfer, Production Editor, who created this fresh new format.

- All my many wonderful readers and clients around the world who have used this workbook year after year and have shared their stories, ideas, and suggestions. Your shared insights have been used in the past editions and continue to be valuable once again in this latest edition.

- Carol Park, my professional colleague and friend, who continues to inspire me with her work, ideas, and strong determination. Mariette and Roger Kennedy and Rosalyn McCambridge for their valuable insight and input. Marcia and Gary Kons, the two most loving, supportive, encouraging, and wise friends anyone could be blessed to have. Their shared physical and emotional strength literally helped me move, on many levels, to the ideal place and situation to write many new editions.

- Cheryl Laures, my whole body balancing "sherpa," whose wisdom and guidance gave me the strength and clarity to follow my path to authentic self and spiritual mastery to share with others.

- And again to my dear New Zealand friends Jessica, Misha, Inga, Ans, and Althea and my other beautiful Quest sisters whose healing wisdom and love will always be a part of who I am and each new book I write.

Recommended Reading

The following books and other resources are included because of their total focus or special sections on *budgeting, credit, debt, spending, money attitudes,* and/or *recovery issues.* If you want more financial planning information, there are numerous excellent books with a full range and comprehensive coverage of all facets of personal finance available at your local book stores, library, or through the Web.

If managing money is new for you, these books offer a variety of ideas, approaches, and information to help you get started. The following books can provide complementary information as you do the practical hands-on part with *The Budget Kit: Common Cent$ Money Management Workbook.*

7 Steps to a 720 Credit Score, Philip X. Tirone (Mortgage Capital Advisors, 2006).

The 9 Steps to Financial Freedom: Practical and Spiritual Steps So You Can Stop Worrying, Suze Orman (Three Rivers Press, 2006).

10 Minute Guide to Beating Debt, Susan Abentrod (Howell Book House, 1996).

Ask and It Is Given: Learning to Manifest Your Desires, Esther and Jerry Hicks (Hay House, Inc, 2005).

Become Totally Debt-Free in Five Years or Less, Gwendolyn D. Gabriel, et al. (Brown Bag Press, 2000).

Bounce Back from Bankruptcy, Paula Langguth Ryan (Pellingham Casper Communications, 2007)

The Complete Idiot's Guide to Personal Finance in Your 20s and 30s, Sarah Young Fisher, Susan Shelly, and Grace W. Weinstein (Alpha Books, 2005).

Conscious Spending for Couples: Seven Skills for Financial Harmony, Deborah Knuckey (Wiley, John & Sons, Inc. 2002).

Consuming Passions: Help for Compulsive Shoppers, Ellen Mohr Catalano (New Harbinger Publications, 1993).

Creating Money: Keys to Abundance, Sanaya Roman and Duane Packer (H.J. Kramer Inc., 1992).

Credit, Cash, and Co-Dependency: The Money Connection, Yvonne Kaye, PhD (Islewest Publishing, 1998).

Credit Card Debt: Reduce Your Financial Burden in Three Easy Steps, Alexander Daskaloff (HarperCollins Publishers, 1999).

The Credit Repair Handbook: Everything You Need to Know to Maintain, Rebuild, and Protect Your Credit, John Ventura (Kaplan Publishing, 2007).

Credit Smart: Your Step-by-Step Guide to Establishing or Reestablishing Good Credit, Gudrun Maria Nickel (Sphinx Publishing, 2003).

Currency of Hope, Debtors Anonymous General Service Board of Trustees, Inc. (1999).

Deal with Your Debt: The Right Way to Manage Your Bills and Pay Off What You Owe, Liz Pulliam Weston (Prentice Hall, 2005).

Debt Free by 30: Practical Advice for the Young, Broke, & Upwardly Mobile, Jason Anthony and Karl Cluck (Plume, 2001).

Debt-Proof Living: The Complete Guide to Living Financially Free, Mary Hunt (DPL Press, Inc., 2006).

Don't Waste Money, Spend It!: Come Join Renowned Tightwad Lisa Wysocki in Her Madcap Adventures in Thriftiness and Frugality, Lisa Wysocki (iUniverse, 2004).

"Don't Worry About a Thing Dear": Why Women Need Financial Intimacy, Helga Hayes (PrimeLife Publishing, 2006).

The Energy of Money: A Spiritual Guide to Financial and Personal Fulfillment, Maria Nemeth, Ph.D. (Wellspring/Ballantine, 2000).

The Everything Budgeting Book, Tere Drenth (Adams Media Corporation, 2003).

The Family Financial Workbook: A Practical Guide to Budgeting, Larry Burkett (Moody Publishers, 2002).

Financial Peace Planner: A Step-by-Step Guide to Restoring Your Family's Financial Health, Dave Ramsey (Penguin Books, 1998).

For Richer, Not Poorer: The Money Book for Couples, Ruth L. Hayden (Health Communications Inc., 1999).

The Frugal Senior: Hundreds of Creative Ways To Stretch A Dollar! (A Best Half of Life Book), Rich Gray (Quill Driver Books, 2005).

The Get Out of Debt Kit: Your Roadmap to Total Financial Freedom, Deborah McNaughton (Kaplan Business, 2002).

Girl, Get Your Money Straight! A Sister's Guide to Healing Your Bank Account and Funding Your Dreams in 7 Simple Steps, Glinda Bridgforth (Broadway Books, 2002).

Got money? Enjoy It! Manage It! Even Save Some of It—Financial Advice for Your Twenties and Thirties!, Jeff Wuorio (Amacom, 1999).

How to Get Out of Debt, Stay Out of Debt & Live Prosperously, Jerrold Mundis (Bantam Books, 2003). Based on the proven principles and techniques of Debtors Anonymous.

How to Have More Than Enough: A Step-by-Step Guide to Creating Abundance, Ten Proven Keys to Increasing Your Wealth and Family Harmony, Dave Ramsey (Penguin Books, 2000).

How to Survive without a Salary: Learning How to Live the Conserver Lifestyle, Charles Long (Warwick Publishers, 2003).

Invest in Yourself: Six Secrets to a Rich Life, Marc Eisenson, Gerri Detweiler, and Nancy Castleman (John Wiley and Sons, 2001).

I Shop, Therefore I Am: Compulsive Buying and the Search for Self, April Lane Benson (Jason Aronson, 2000).*

Joyfully Debt Free: How to Get Out of Debt, Stay Out, and Accumulate a Fortune!, John D. Floyd (Trafford Publishing, 2007).

Life after Debt: Free Yourself from the Burden of Money Worries Once and for All, Bob Hammond (Career Press, 2000).

Miserly Moms: Living on One Income in a Two-Income Economy, Jonni McCoy (Bethany House, 2003).

Money Advice for Your Successful Remarriage: Handling Delicate Financial Issues with Love and Understanding, Patricia Schiff Estess (ASJA Press, 2001).

Money Drunk, Money Sober: 90 Days to Financial Freedom, Mark Bryan and Julia Cameron (Wellspring/Ballantine, 1999).

Money for Life: Budgeting Success and Financial Fitness in Just 12 Weeks, Steven B. Smith (In2M Corporation, 2007).

Money Habitudes—A Deck of Cards that Helps People Understand their Relationship with Money, Syble Solomon (http://www.lifewise.us/moneyhabitudes/).

Money Harmony: Resolving Money Conflicts in Your Life and Relationships, Olivia Mellan (Walker & Company, 1995).

The Motley Fool Personal Finance Workbook: A Foolproof Guide to Organizing Your Cash and Building Wealth, David Gardner, et al. (Fireside, 2002).

Overcoming Overspending: A Winning Plan for Spenders and Their Partners, Olivia Mellan (Walker and Company, 1997).

Overcoming Underearning: Overcome Your Money Fears and Earn What You Deserve, Barbara Stanny (Collins, 2005).

Penny Pinching: How to Lower Your Everyday Expenses without Lowering Your Standard of Living, Lee and Barbara Simmons (Bantam Books, 1999).

---

*NOTE: considering the issue and the price, I recommend you find a copy at the library or a used copy.

Personal Finance for Dummies (5th Edition), Eric Tyson (For Dummies, 2005).

The Pocket Idiot's Guide to Living on a Budget, Peter J. Sander and Jennifer Basye Sander (Alpha Books, 2005).

Prince Charming Isn't Coming: How Women Get Smart About Money, Barbara Stanny (Penguin, 2007).

Prospering Woman: A Complete Guide to Achieving the Full Abundant Life, Ruth Ross, PhD (New World Library, 1995).

Quick and Easy Budget Book, Dianna Barra (Idea Designs LLC, 2002).

Rich Dad Poor Dad for Teens: The Secrets about Money—That You Don't Learn in School! (Rich Dad Poor Dad), Robert T. Kiyosaki and Sharon L. Lechter (Little, Brown Young Readers, 2004).

Richest Man in Babylon, George S. Clason (Signet, 2002).

Secrets of the Millionaire Mind: Mastering the Inner Game of Wealth, T. Harv Eker (HarperCollins Publishers, 2005).

Simple Money Solutions: 10 Ways You Can Stop Feeling Overwhelmed by Money and Start Making It Work for You, Nancy Lloyd (Crown Business, 2001).

Slash Your Debt: Save Money and Secure Your Future—Winning Debt Consolidation Strategies From America's Top Credit Experts, Gerri Detweiler, Marc Eisenson, and Nancy Casleman (Financial Literacy Center, 2006).

Suze Orman's Financial Guidebook: Put the 9 Steps to Work, Suze Orman (Three Rivers Press, 2002).

The Total Money Makeover: A Proven Plan for Financial Fitness, Dave Ramsey (Thomas Nelson Publishers, 2007).

The Ultimate Credit Handbook: How to Double Your Credit, Cut Your Debt, and Have a Lifetime of Great Credit (3rd Edition), Gerri Detweiler (Plume, 2003).

Your Credit Score: How to Fix, Improve, and Protect the 3-Digit Number that Shapes Your Financial Future, Liz Pulliam Weston (FT Press, 2007).

Zero Debt: The Ultimate Guide to Financial Freedom, Lynnette Khalfani (Advantage World Press, 2004).

Zero Debt for College Grads: From Student Loans to Financial Freedom, Lynette Khalfani (Kaplan Publishing, 2007).

Online Resources

Now, with such an abundance of online information, the real skill is using effective searching techniques for finding the most helpful information. The other skill is to be discerning about the accuracy, value, and security of the information and websites you do find and actually use.

Rather than spending endless hours doing a keyword search on the major search engines, I recommend starting out with the websites listed in this section. They all have a phenomenal amount of valuable information and have a primary focus or informative section on general basic money management with topics covering, but not limited to, the following:

- Budgeting
- Credit
- Credit cards
- Debt
- Spending
- Spending guidelines
- Saving money
- Money attitudes
- Recovery issues

Many of these websites provide excellent articles, books, and online newsletters—often for free or discounted.

There are also now hundreds of convenient and well-designed calculators at various websites for developing basic budgets, calculating debt payoff or savings, and determining loan terms and total costs.

Other websites offer special debt management counseling and payment services. Be cautious as you explore these particular companies, even if they are listed as nonprofit. See "Getting Online Help" on *page* 103 for a review of what to expect for legitimate debt management services.

If this endless amount of information seems overwhelming, one way to narrow down your search efficiently is by going to the larger portals, which are all-inclusive sites. A few of these large services, like MSN, AOL, and Yahoo! are marked with asterisks "**". The website address provided in the list below should take you directly to the personal finance section and save you a few layers of searching. If you do start on the home page, search around for the buttons, words, or tabs that indicate titles like "Money," "Budgets," "Personal Finance," "Family Finance," "Planning," "Consumer Credit or Debt," and "Education" to get you started. You often will find a motherlode of articles archived by topic and/or author. Most of these articles are written and researched by some of the top financial authors and experts in the country.

Nearly every article and website you view will have a host of additional related links to keep your search moving.

About.com
about.com/money

American Consumer Credit Counseling
www.consumercredit.com/index.html

American Savings Education Council
www.asec.org

**AOL Money and Finance
money.aol.com/pfhub

Bankrate.com—Independent financial information
www.bankrate.com/brm/news/news_finance_home.asp

Better Budgeting
www.betterbudgeting.com

Card Ratings
cardratings.com

Choose to Save Education Program
www.choosetosave.org

**CNN Money
money.cnn.com/pf/index.html

Consumer Credit Counseling Services
www.cccsintl.org

Credit Line Financial
www.creditline.org

Dave Ramsey
www.daveramsey.com

Debtors Anonymous—12 Step
www.debtorsanonymous.com

The Dollar Stretcher: Living Better for Less
www.stretcher.com

Family Resource Center
www.ourfamilyplace.com

Federal Consumer Information Center
www.pueblo.gsa.gov

Financial Planning: Complete Guide to Personal Finance and Financial Success
www.financialplan.about.com

Finish Rich Resource Center
www.finishrich.com/free_resources/fr_lattefactor.php

**Fox News
www.foxnews.com/business/index.html

Genus Credit Management
www.myafs.org

Good Advice Press/The Pocket Change Investor NL
www.goodadvicepress.com

Institute of Consumer Financial Education
www.financial-education-icfe.org

Kiplinger Magazine Online
www.kiplinger.com

Mary Hunt's Debt Proof Living
www.cheapskatemonthly.com

Miserly Moms
www.miserlymoms.com

**MoneyCentral MSN Saving and Spending
moneycentral.msn.com/planning/home.asp

**MSN Money
moneycentral.msn.com/home.asp

Mvelopes™ Personal
www.moneytracker.mvelopes.com

Myvesta.org Nonprofit Financial Help
www.myvesta.org

National Foundation for Consumer Credit
www.nfcc.org

Oprah.com
www.oprah.com/money/money_landing.jhtml

Personal Budgeting and Money Saving Tips
personal-budget-planning-saving-money.com/index.html

Right On the Money
www.rightonthemoney.org

Smart Money
www.smartmoney.com/pf/?nav=dropTab

US Financial Literacy and Education Commission
http://mymoney.gov

**USA Today
www.usatoday.com/money/default.htm

Women's Institute for Financial Education
www.wife.org

Womens Wall Street
www.womenswallstreet.com/Default.aspx

**Yahoo! Finance Education Center Managing Debt
biz.yahoo.com/edu/ed_debt.html

finance.yahoo.com/personal-finance

YOUNG MONEY Magazine
www.youngmoney.com

INDEX

About The Author

Judy **Lawrence, MS Ed**., is a financial counselor and popular speaker and workshop facilitator on basic money management. She has been a featured guest on numerous television and radio shows throughout the country and quoted in a variety of publications for over two decades. *The Budget Kit* was originally developed in 1981 as *Common Cent$: The Complete Money Management Workbook* and was a true pioneer in the early days of limited personal financial management books.

As a result of her various experiences of being a REALTOR®, college rep, and counselor at a Boarding School on the Navajo Reservation and a large technical college, Judy saw the need for a nonintimidating workbook that could immediately be used by people with limited time or limited organizing and budgeting skills. Her foresight then during the "low-tech" era of the early 1980s is just as timely now in this high-tech information-age 21st century.

She launched a unique financial budget counseling practice in Albuquerque, New Mexico, where she counseled couples, individuals, and small businesses, and later expanded her business to become a family law court-appointed expert developing and evaluating personal budgets. Her techniques and workbooks, including *The Money Tracker, The Family Memory Book, and Daily Riches Gratitude Journal*, have all focused on providing valuable information and basic, encouraging, and extremely user-friendly support.

Judy now lives in Cupertino, California, where she continues to have a national consulting practice by phone and e-mail. Living in the heart of the Silicon Valley, she continues to explore innovative ways to make a difference.

You can visit Judy's website at *www.moneytracker.com* or arrange directly for media interviews, speaking engagements, or telephone consultations by calling 408-747-9589 or by email at judy@moneytracker.com.

ATTENTION MS EXCEL USERS

As a value-added service, it is now possible to combine the simplicity of the traditional manual worksheet with the technology of immediate calculations. Available in the exact same format as the workbook are the three worksheets with the most calculations: The Monthly Expense Record, The Monthly Budget Worksheet, and The Yearly Budget Worksheet. All totals are calculated automatically, saving you hours of manual calculator time. Visit for more information. *http://moneytracker.com/book-TheBudgetKitExcel.htm*